MAY 3 2013
CS

LORIMER FIELD GUIDE TO 225

ONTARIO
BIRDS

Written and illustrated by
JEFFREY C. DOMM

Birding listings by Ted Cheskey, Pete Read, Mike Street,
Hugh Currie and Ron Tozer

WITHD D1250323

James Lorimer & Company Ltd., Publishers
Toronto

COLDSTREAM PUBLIC LIBRARY

Copyright © 2012 by Jeffrey C. Domm

All rights reserved. No part of this book may be reproduced or transmitted in any form or by any means, electronic or mechanical, including photocopying, or by any information storage or retrieval system, without permission in writing from the publisher.

James Lorimer & Company Ltd., Publishers acknowledges the support of the Ontario Arts Council. We acknowledge the financial support of the Government of Canada through the Canada Book Fund for our publishing activities. We acknowledge the support of the Canada Council for the Arts which last year invested $24.3 million in writing and publishing throughout Canada. We acknowledge the Government of Ontario through the Ontario Media Development Corporation's Ontario Book Initiative.

Library and Archives Canada Cataloguing in Publication

Domm, Jeffrey C., 1958-
    Lorimer field guide to 225 Ontario birds / Jeffrey C. Domm.

    Includes index.
       Previous ed. published under title: Lorimer pocketguide to Ontario birds.
    Issued also in an electronic format.

ISBN 978-1-4594-0041-2

    1. Birds--Ontario--Identification. 2. Bird watching--Ontario--Guidebooks. I. Title.

QL685.5.O5D63 2012   598.09713   C2011-908456-2

James Lorimer & Company Ltd., Publishers
317 Adelaide Street West, Suite 1002
Toronto, ON
M5V 1P9
www.lorimer.ca

Printed and bound in China

Contents

Introduction

Southern Ontario is an excellent place to enjoy birdwatching. A rich mosaic of forest, meadow, river, lake, marsh, and beach, it is home to a wide variety of breeding birds and year-round residents, and is part of the migration path for dozens of other species on their seasonal journeys between breeding and wintering grounds. In summer and fall, hundreds of species can be identified around the province, many of them in full mating plumage.

It can be difficult to identify wild birds correctly, especially if they are a great distance away and foliage or other obstacles are blocking your view. The full-colour illustrations in this book, along with the visual keys and the descriptions, will help you quickly compare essential features.

Each illustration has been drawn especially for this guide from photographs, live observations, scientific specimens, and written descriptions. They represent typical specimens. When comparing a bird with the illustration, one has to bear in mind that plumage varies from individual to individual. Many birds change plumage seasonally and the colours change in different light conditions.

This book is divided into two sections: Water Birds and Land Birds. Within each section, the birds are arranged into groups such as gulls, raptors, or warblers, and birds that are of similar type and size are in close proximity.

Of the hundreds of birds that either reside in or pass through southern Ontario, a selection of 225 familiar species was chosen for this book. In addition to the very common and widespread birds, there are those that have limited habitat but are of great interest to birdwatching enthusiasts. Birds that breed in Ontario are identified by an accurate illustration of their egg. The list of Birding Hot Spots (pages 12–26), updated by Ted Cheskey, Manager of bird conservation programs for Nature Canada; Pete Read, freelance bird biologist for environmental assessments in Ontario; and and Ron Tozer, author and former Park Naturalist in Algonquin Provincial Park, will guide you to accessible areas across southern Ontario that experienced birdwatchers have found to be excellent birding sites.

Before setting out on a birdwatching trip, be sure to dress warmly and watch the weather. High winds or a sudden drop in temperature can affect the number of birds you see, as well as dampen your spirits if you are not well prepared. Experienced birders also recommend you leave your valuables at home and lock your car doors before you leave it to go birding.

With the help of this guide you will find that birdwatching is both rewarding and full of surprises. As you begin to recognize many of the birds of eastern North America, you will appreciate their abundant variety.

How to Use This Guide

Birds don't stay in one place for very long, so it is important to learn a few simple rules to help you quickly identify them. You will often see waterfowl or shorebirds either feeding or flying. If a bird is on the water, you can watch to see if it dives, skims the surface, or tips its head underwater, leaving its tail feathers pointing to the sky. If it is flying, you can observe the beating pattern of its wings — are they quick wingbeats, is it soaring, or does it flap its wings and then glide?

Viewing land birds is a bit different. Most often what you see is a bird that is feeding; perhaps it is hopping along the ground or flitting from branch to branch. Maybe it is perched in a tree, preparing to fly away.

The visual keys given in this guide focus on the primary identifiable features of each bird, and include colour, outline, and size. Because water birds are more often seen in flight than land birds, and have a wider variety of food-gathering methods, we have also included flying pattern and feeding style.

Secondary features for both kinds of birds include foot type, egg colour and size, and observation calendar.

When you are looking at a bird, first estimate the size, then take note of the shape of the wings, tail, head, bill or beak, and feet. Note any particular marks — patches, streaks, stripes, and speckles. Finally, observe its movements.

Legend for visual keys

① Size identification — the rectangle represents the page of this book, and the silhouette of the bird represents its size against this page.

② Foot type — Tridactyl

Anisodactyl   Zygodactyl

③ Flight characteristics —

Quick wingbeats

Slow, steady wingbeats

Soaring

Wingbeats followed by gliding

Category of Bird

①

Size Identification

②

Foot Type

③

Flight Characteristics

4 **Feeding technique** —

Stabs and prodding motion

Grazing and dabbling

Diving head first

Dives from water's surface

Tip up feeding

Skims water surface

5 **Egg** — actual size and shape unless otherwise indicated.

6 **Backyard feeder** — there are three types of bird feeders to which small birds might be attracted.

7 **Birdhouse nester** — some species are happy to make their nest in a manmade house, which you might hang in your garden.

8 **Nesting location** (for inland birds only)

▼ Hollow in ground

▼ Waterside plants

▽ Bushes and thickets

▼ Cavities of trees

▼ Deciduous trees

▼ Conifers and tall trees

▼ Tall, dead, decaying trees

▼ Banks along rivers and ponds

▽ Cliffs and/or rocky ledges

9 **Observation calendar** — the bar gives the initial for each of the twelve months of the year. The deeper colour indicates the best months for seeing the species, according to known migration patterns.

Observation Calendar

vii

Feeding Technique

Egg

Backyard Feeder

Birdhouse Nester

Nesting Location

Quick Reference Index

Step 1: Determine the approximate size of bird in relation to page size.

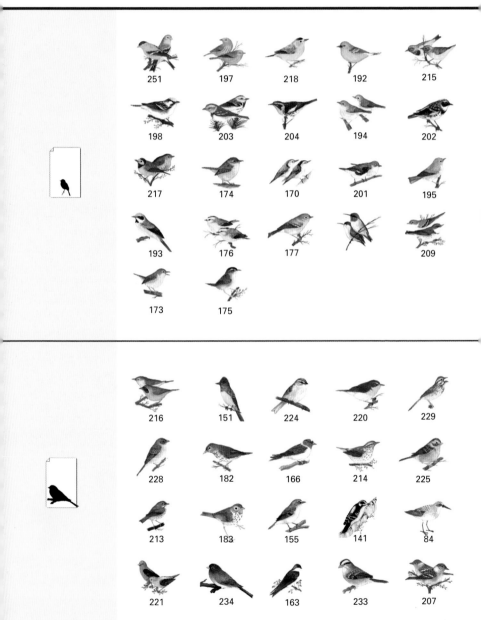

Step 2: Compare overall colour and specific markings and turn to the page number.

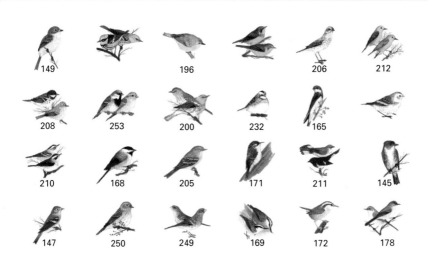

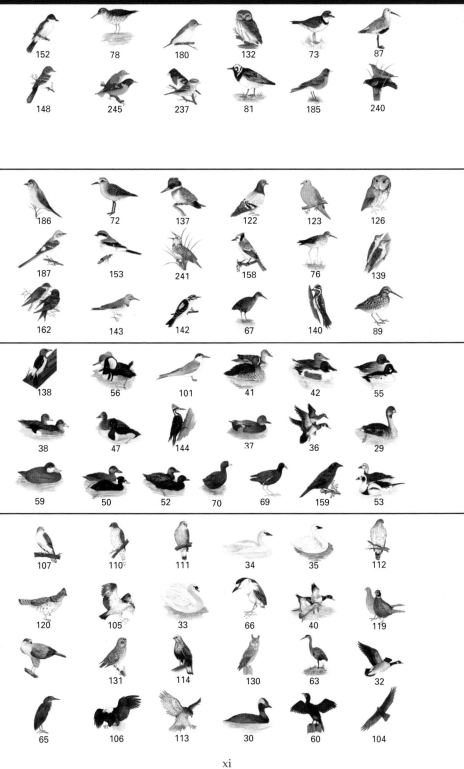

Birding Hot Spots

"Hot spots" are the sites experienced birders identify as the best places to observe birds in the wild. Below are one hundred of Southern Ontario's hottest birding spots, selected by Ted Cheskey, Pete Read, and Ron Tozer. Many of these hotspots are Important Bird Areas (IBA). IBA is a program of BirdLife International, a global partnership for bird conservation, and, serves to identify the most important sites for birds on earth. Approximately six hundred are recognized in Canada, of which Ontario has seventy. To learn more about IBAs visit www.ibacanada.ca. IBAs are marked with an asterisk. Please consult a current provincial road map for directions or contact hot-spot sites directly for information on access and entry fees. For those seeking to do more than just go birding, consider participating in one of dozens of Christmas Bird Counts held across the province between December 14 and January 3 each year, or volunteering at one of the several bird observatories in Ontario where migration monitoring, including bird banding, is conducted.

Please note that wherever possible, a street address has been provided, which can be readily found by GPS or using online maps. In cases where a street address does not exist, descriptive directions are provided.

Southwestern Ontario
Birding hot spots selected by Ted Cheskey

1 Grand Bend
Pinery Provincial Park – Port Franks*
This is an excellent park for access to Lake Huron. It is a great place to bird, either on the trails through the oak-savannah habitat, or by looking out on the lake. It is good for nesting species such as Tufted Titmouse, Rose-breasted Grosbeak, and many others, but also for migrants and winter birds. Eight kilometres south of Grand Bend on Highway 21, at 9526 Lakeshore Road. Expect user fees in season.

2 Kettle Point*
This is an excellent location in the fall to observe migrating loons and waterfowl. During migration watch for migrating land birds including winter finches, snow buntings, horned larks, Lapland longspurs, and waxwings in mid to late fall along the network of forested cottage roads. Thirty-five kilometres northeast of Sarnia. 6247 Indian Lane, RR2 Lambton Shores.

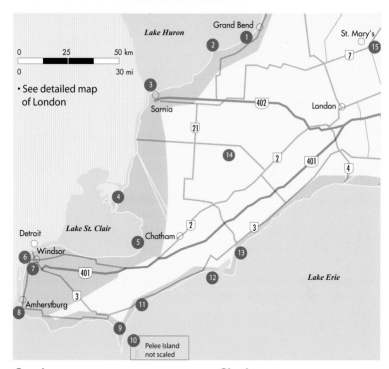

Sarnia

3 Point Edward*

The lighthouse marks the outlet of Lake Huron into the St. Clair River, where waterfowl, gulls, and the occasional jaeger species are funnelled after a strong cold front in the fall. Don't forget to check for land birds!

4 Walpole Island*

This huge delta prairie and wetland has amazing birds. Egrets, herons, ducks, rails and coots, grasslands and savannah species can be found. You will need to hire a guide for access to the most interesting locations.

Chatham

5 St. Clair National Wildlife Area and Eastern Lake St. Clair*

A system of dykes and viewing towers allows access to marshes rich in wetland birds. Rails, herons, egrets, waterfowl, and Bald Eagles can be observed in the spring, summer, or fall. Black-bellied Plovers and Lesser Golden Plovers stop in fields between Bradley and Mitchell's Bay in early to mid May and Tundra Swans can be seen in March. The St. Clair National Wildlife Area is bounded by the Municipality of Chatham-Kent's Townline Road and Balmoral Line.

Windsor

6 **Detroit River***

In the fall, winter, and early spring, large numbers of waterfowl, including Canvasback and Redhead, congregate along the Detroit River, easily observed from parkland.

7 **Ojibwa Prairie**

In southwest Windsor, the Ojibwa prairie provides a mix of woodlands and prairie where southern species such as Carolina Wren and many migrants can be observed. The Ojibwa Nature Centre is at 5200 Matchette Road.

Amherstburg

8 **Holiday Beach Conservation Area***

Best known for migrating hawks that pass over the park in the fall, some days in the thousands, this hot spot is spectacular during all seasons. Wetlands, woodlands, shoreline, and a viewing platform make for great birding. Plan for a visit in early to mid September that coincides with the first cold front with north winds. 6952 Essex County Road 50, Amherstburg.

Point Pelee

9 **Point Pelee National Park***

One of the top birding sites in North America, Pelee's birding peaks in May when trees can drip with warblers, tanagers, vireos, and grosbeaks, and the ground can move with thrushes and sparrows. Watch for Red-breasted Merganser on the lake and check the tip for gulls and shorebirds. Sewage lagoons north of the park can be great for shorebirds. Essex County Road 33 at Mersea Road East.

10 **Pelee Island***

The short ferry trip to Pelee Island from Kingsville or Leamington is well worth taking. A mixture of open woods, farms, vineyards, and nature reserves, Pelee Island offers great opportunities for birding combined with biking. Watch for Yellow-breasted Chat, cuckoos and migrants in the spring. Check MV Jiimaan listings at www.ontarioferries.com for schedule information.

11 **Wheatley Provincial Park**

Birding and camping within the park are excellent in May, when many species of warblers and flycatchers, Scarlet Tanager, Rose-breasted Grosbeak, Indigo Bunting, and many other species stop in the vegetation. A trip to Hillman Marsh will add a great number of water birds and shorebirds! 21116 Klondyke Road, Wheatley.

Rondeau Bay

12 **Erieau***

The harbour hums with gulls and terns in the spring and fall. Check for Forster's and Common Terns and Bonaparte's Gulls. The McGeachy Pond Conservation Area just northwest of town on Erieau Road is rich in water birds and shorebirds.

⑬ Rondeau Provincial Park*

The endangered Prothonotary Warbler nests in the lowland swamp forests. A good trail system through forest and coastal wetlands makes birding in the spring extremely productive. Rondeau Bay is one of the best waterfowl viewing locations on the Great Lakes in late March and April. On Wildwood Line, south from the junction of Highways 15 and 17.

Newbury

⑭ Middlesex County Forests / Skunk's Misery*

South of Newbury, on county road 14 (Concession Drive) are hundreds of hectares of public and private forest with breeding Wood Thrush, Red-eyed Vireo, Eastern Pewee, Rose-breasted Grosbeak, American Redstarts and threatened species such as Hooded Warbler, Cerulean Warbler and Acadian Flycatcher. Be prepared for mosquitoes in the spring. A user-management plan is in the works and there are many proposed access trails off several roads in the area roughly bounded by Concession Road in the north, Trillium Road in the south, Hagerty Road in the east, and Sassafras Road in the west. Keep off posted lands and take along boots for the wet trails and insect repellent in bug season.

St. Mary's

⑮ Wildwood Conservation Area

Visible from Highway 7 at the intersection with County Road 9 (Perth Line), seven kilometres east of St. Marys, this large reservoir attracts ducks such as Mallard, American Black Duck, Ring-necked Duck, Lesser Scaup, Bufflehead, and mergansers. Large numbers of gulls roost on the reservoir.

London

Birding hot spots selected by Pete Read

① 1. Fanshawe Park Conservation Area

This is a recreation-class park, with camping and many other facilities. In migration periods, waterfowl use the large artificial lake above the dam. Songbirds are found throughout the Park during migration on the various well-marked trails which are located on maps on site. The evergreen plantations within the park sometimes hold wintering finches and crossbills. Expect user fees in season. 1424 Clarke Road.

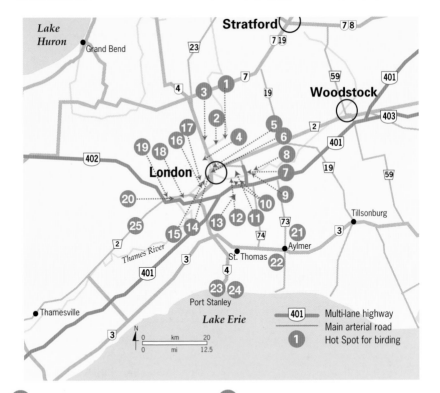

2 Thames Valley Trail

This long trail follows the Thames river, often along both sides. Many resident riverside birds, such as Catbird, House Wren, Baltimore Oriole and others, nest along the trails. In spring and fall, the river acts as a migration corridor for birds. The trails can be accessed by many spots. On the north branch, one north-side access is located at the end of Windermere Road, off Adelaide Street between Kipp's Lane and Fanshawe Road. There is a southside access off Kilally Road. Take Kilally Road west from Highbury Avenue. There is a trail fro Edgevalley Road to the river.

3 Weldon Park

This little park has good trails that cut through mixed habitat. These trails can be rewarding, especially during migration, but also during the winter when some birds use the park for food and shelter. Red-bellied Woodpecker and Eastern Wood-Peewee are found in the upland woods. 21466 Richmond Street, Arva (access from St. Drive).

4 Medway Valley

This is an Environmentally Significant Area, located along the Medway River and running between Fanshaw Park Road and Western Road. Various habitats are seen along its trails. Look for resident birds like Downy Woodpecker and Belted Kingfisher, but also watch for migrants, especially warbler species in mid-May. Best access is on a trail from the west side of the parking lot of the London Museum of Archaeology, 1600 Attawandaron Road.

5 **Gibbons Park / UWO campus**
Popular trails follow the river through this park and up to the University of Western Ontario. Resident birds include Baltimore Oriole, Mallard, swallows, and sometimes Great Blue Heron. Enter off Grosvenor or Victoria.

6 **Harris Park**
This little park is a groomed, well-used spot, located where the north and south branches of the Thames River meet. At all times of the year, look for waterfowl in the river, just off the parking area below the art gallery. Riverside Drive becomes Dundas Street as you head east, and you can access the park by turning left immediately after crossing the bridge.

7 **South Branch Bikeway**
This long path goes through many different habitats as it follows the south branch of the Thames River for about eight kilometres, alternating

on the north and south banks. Look for migrant species in spring and residents such as Cardinal, Gray Catbird and Red-winged Blackbird. Two good spots for birds are the first section from the Pottersburg Treatment Plant, where parking is off Hamilton Road, just east of Gore Road, to the Highbury bridge and between the Egerton Street bridge and Adelaide bridge, on either side of the river.

8 **Kiwanis Park**
The park runs along a creek that empties into the Thames. Paths wander through the various habitats. Look for Eastern Phoebe, Northern Cardinal, and Kingfisher, as well as migrants in spring and fall. Park in the small parking area beside the Gore Road bridge over the creek. Then walk north along the trail on the west side of the Pottersburg Creek. Watch out for trains as you scramble up the embankment and drop down to the other side of the creek. Continue down the other side following paths back to Gore Road.

9 **Meadowlily Woods**
This Environmentally Significant Area is about forty-six hectares of public land with trails leading down to old growth Maple / Beech woodlands along the south branch of the Thames. It is

known for migrating birds (especially warblers) in mid-May, but you can see resident woodland species like Scarlet Tanager, Rose-breasted Grosbeak and Red-bellied Woodpecker. It is located on Meadowlily Road, off Commissioner's Road East, just west of the intersection with Highbury. Park near the gates called "Park Farms," and walk left on the path. There is privately owned land there also, so watch for and obey any signs.

10 Westminster Ponds / Pond Mills Conservation Area

This is a very large and habitat-rich area stretching from Pond Mills Conservation Area through a creek valley to Westminster Ponds Conservation Area. The first has two kettle lakes (Ice-Age deep, small lakes) on the east end, while the second has three kettle lakes. Resident Great Horned Owl, Song Sparrow, Black-capped Chickadee, Northern Cardinal, and many others are found here. It is one of the best places in the London area to see migrant species, from waterfowl in the lakes to warblers in the woods. Pond Mills Conservation Area can be accessed from near the intersection of Southdale Road and Pond Mills Road. For Westminster Ponds, you can park at the back of the London

Tourist Information Centre, 696 Wellington Road South. It is best to cover these places separately, parking at either end and enjoying the sets of ponds.

11 The Coves

This is an area of three ponds that are an oxbow of the Thames River. Besides the one on the Greenway side mentioned above, there are two others on the south side of the road, with natural areas around them. Many riverside species such as Northern Cardinal, Gray Catbird, and Carolina Wren can be found nesting there, and it can have many migrant passerines in the spring and fall. To access the pond north of Springbank Drive see the part on Greenway. To access the trails on the south side there are several spots but best is off of Cove Road, which runs west off Wharncliffe Road S., two streets east of the intersection with Springbank Drive.

12 Highland Woods

A naturalized area bordering the south-western edge of the Highland Golf and Country Club. Mixed wet deciduous/coniferous woods host many vernal ponds and give way to open meadows with habitat for many species of birds, especially during migration. In nesting season look for American Goldfinch and House Wren. Access is off Rossmore Court. From Wharncliffe Road S. and Commissioner's Road, travel south on Wharncliffe, then east on the first road, Highview Avenue. Follow Highview as it curves and go east on Rossmore Court. Parking is on the road. Look for the walkway on your left to enter.

13 Kirk-Cousins Management Area

This is a productive birding area with varied habitat to wander through. From the parking lot, walk the trails or scan the area from the viewing stands overlooking the ponds to see waterfowl and herons. Migrants, such as warblers, and nesting species, such as Wood Thrush, use the woods. Kirk-Cousins is on Scotland Drive, just east of the intersection with Wellington Road South.

14 Greenway Park

This is a large park where hiking trails give access upstream and down on the river. Especially in the winter, look for waterfowl and gull species in the warm spillwater from the Greenway Pollution Plant near the building. Or walk over to the small oxbow pond close to Springbank that may have Gray Catbird in the trees, or Blue Heron in its shallow waters. Parking is accessed off Springbank Drive onto Greenside Avenue. Not in

the park but on the other side of the river, a trail follows the river from Cavendish Crescent westward to Wonderland Road. Cavendish is reached from Riverside Drive, just west of the intersection at Wharncliffe Road.

15 Springbank Park

An old park with large trees, Springbank has many walking trails that follow the river. In summer, Springbank has Gray Catbird, Song Sparrow, Northern Cardinal, Yellow Warbler, American Goldfinch. Along the river it is also home to Mallard Duck, Red-winged Blackbird, Common Yellowthroat, Belted Kingfisher and Great Blue Heron. It is a good winter spot for waterfowl and gulls. Park off Springbank Drive and walk in from the east entrance, or go farther west and make a turn west onto Commissioner's Road West, to the entrance off that street.

16 Warbler Woods

This Environmentally Significant Area consists of hilly woodlands of mainly old-growth forest, and contains typical woodland species, such as Wood Thrush, Rose-breasted Grosbeak, and American Robin. In May, watch for many migrants, especially warblers. American Redstart, Common Yellowthroat, and Yellow Warbler may be found nesting in or near the woods. The parking area is found on the left just as you ascend the hill heading west on Commissioner's Road West, out of Byron, a community at the west edge of London.

17 Sifton Bog

A remnant of the Ice Age, this acidic bog is rare habitat in southern Ontario. There is a boardwalk onto the bog for viewing and trails in the surrounding woods nearby. Besides special flora (including leatherleaf and pitcher plant) around the little sphagnum-covered lake, look for resident species, which include American Robin, Black-capped Chickadee, and Common Yellowthroat. Parking is in a small lot off the south side of Oxford Street West, just west of the intersection with Hyde Park Road.

18 Komoka Provincial Park

Located along the Thames River at the west edge of London, this large park is mostly a nature preserve with many trails through varied habitat. The bird list comprises about 80 nesting species, including Blue-winged Warbler, Brown Thrasher, Eastern Towhee, and, in the woods, Scarlet Tanager, Blue Jay, and others. Savannah, Grasshopper, and Field sparrows as well as other field nesters live in the old

gravel pit on the north side. Riverside species such as Song Sparrow and Cardinal can also be found. This park is also especially good for spring and fall migrants. To access the south side, there are two main parking areas.

19 Komoka Ponds

These old gravel-pit ponds have become resting areas for about 25 species of waterfowl in the spring and fall. Common migrants include American Coot, Ring-necked Duck, wigeon, mergansers, and cormorants. They are located at the northeast corner of the intersection of Komoka Road, Middlesex County Road 16, and Glendon Drive at the lights in Komoka. Glendon is Middlesex County Road 14, an extension of Commissioner's Road West, coming out of London (Byron). Park along either road facing the lake. It is best to bring a viewing scope, as the birds can be far away.

20 Delaware Sportsman Pond

This is a great marsh wetland for herons, Wood Duck, and Red-winged Blackbird, as well as for species in the surrounding woodlands. Listen for Sora and other rails, and perhaps bitterns. Although access is by permission only, there is a good viewing area overlooking the marsh, from Bringham Road, between Gideon

Drive and Longwoods Road. Also known as Middlesex County Road 3, Gideon runs southwest off Commissioner's Road West, heading towards Delaware. Bringham runs south from it, at the corner where the Versa Care nursing home is located.

Aylmer Wildlife Management Area*

This is a great area, with viewing stands, for spotting waterfowl, especially the Tundra Swans that arrive (sometimes by the thousands) in March and early April. Northeast of Aylmer, on Hacienda Road less than a kilometre north of its intersection with Glencolin Line (County Road 32).

Springwater Conservation Area*

A great local birding hot spot. Breeders in the beautiful Carolinian forest include Red-eyed Vireo, Scarlet Tanager, Wood Thrush, and Eastern Wood-Peewee. South on Elgin County Road 35 from Orwell. The main entrance is about three kilometres south of Orwell, on the east side of the road.

Port Stanley and the Port Stanley Lagoons

This is a pretty harbour along Lake Erie and a good spot for migrating waterfowl and gulls. Look out over the lake for ducks and look for rarer gulls, such as Great Black-backed, in the winter. The lagoons are near the port, and one can find many species of waterfowl, gulls, and shorebirds, especially in fall migration. The lagoons and viewing stands are on Scotch Line. Take Carlow Road (Rd 20) north from where it meets George Street just west of the liftbridge to the four-way stop at Warren Street. Turn left, west onto Lake Line, and proceed up the hill to the first road on the right, which is Scotch Line. Turn right onto Scotch and the lagoons are less than a kilometre on the left.

Hawk Cliff*

This hot-spot for hawk migration in the fall should be visited in the second or third week of September, when thousands of hawks pass by on favorable winds, just above the land or high in the sky in "kettles" of raptors. Sharp-shinned and Cooper's Hawks pass at tree-top height, while high overhead you might see a "kettle" of Broad-winged Hawks or, later in the fall, Rough-legged Hawks and Golden Eagles. If you go on one of the locally advertised viewing weekends when banding of the hawks is organized, banders release captives in front of you, as well as answer your questions. Hawk Cliff is at the lake end of Hawk Cliff Road, four kilometres east of Port Stanley.

Longwoods Conservation Area
A variety of habitats are found
in Longwoods, from open
fields to wet woods, ravine
to marsh. It is located west
of London on Longwoods
Road (Middlesex County
Road 2). Here you can find
migrants such as Gray Catbird
in season, while Northern
Cardinal and Black-capped
Chickadee appear all year.
You can also spot marsh birds,
such as Swamp Sparrow
and Red-winged Blackbird.
About five kilometres west
of Delaware on Longwoods
Road. Watch for the entrance
on the north side. Expect user
fees in season.

South-central Ontario
Birding hot spots selected by Ted Cheskey

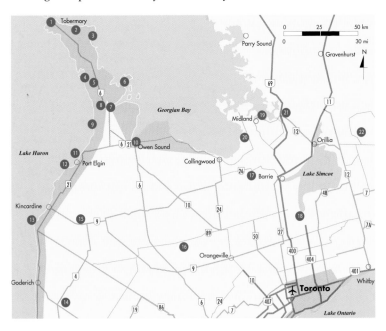

1 Tobermory
Headlands and bays around
Tobermory are migrant traps
in spring and fall; sparrows,
warblers, and other land birds
can be abundant in April
and May. Migrating hawks,
waterfowl, loons, and grebes
can be seen from shoreline
observation points. The back
roads around Tobermory,
including cottage roads near
Lake Huron, can be fantastic
birding locations during
spring migration.

2 Bruce Peninsula National Park
Singing Sands Park, on
the Lake Huron side (take
Dorcas Bay Road west off

Highway 6), provides exciting birding during spring and fall migration and is home to many species of more northern breeding warblers. The Cyprus Lake area (Cyprus Lake Road east off Highway 6) provides good year-round birding. In spring and summer watch and listen for Black-throated Green Warbler, American Redstart, White-throated Sparrow, Hermit and Swainson's Thrush, and Whip-poor-will.

3 Dyer's Bay and Cabot Head*

The pastures and woodlands near Dyer's Bay are rich in open-country species such as Eastern Meadowlark, Brown Thrasher, Eastern Kingbird, Upland Sandpiper, and Eastern Bluebird. Sandhill Cranes and American Bitterns frequent wet fields and wetlands. Check Georgian Bay for grebes, loons, and mergansers, as well as the Cabot Head lighthouse for migrants. Bruce Peninsula Bird Observatory operates a migration monitoring station nearby that requires prior notice for visitation.

4 Stokes Bay

Black Creek Provincial Park, south of Stokes Bay, is a great spring birding destination, with rich mixed forests with many breeding warbler species such as Blackburnian and Black-and-white. In the winter look for northern finches such

as Pine Siskin and White-winged Crossbill.

5 Ferndale Flats

Flat, open farmland south of Ferndale is home to Red-winged Blackbirds, Savannah Sparrows, and Wilson's Snipe in wet areas. In the winter, check for Rough-legged Hawk and Snowy Owl.

6 Cape Croker Indian Park and Campground

On First Nations land, the open prairie along Sydney Bay has breeding Savannah and Grasshopper Sparrows. The forests around the campground have breeding Wood Thrush, Hermit Thrush (dry forest), Veery (damp forest), Rose-breasted Grosbeak, and Eastern Wood Pewees.

7 Wiarton

Colpoy's Bay is worth checking for waterfowl. At Purple Valley, Least Flycatchers, Yellow-bellied Sapsuckers, and hummingbirds nest in the forests, and hawks and Turkey Vulture migrate along the escarpment in the spring. Watch for Ruby-throated Hummingbirds around active Sapsucker drillings.

8 The Rankin River and Isaac Lake

Isaac Lake, west off Highway 6 at Isaac Lake Road (10 km north of Wiarton), harbours breeding Black Terns, Osprey, Wood Ducks, Hooded Mergansers, and Belted Kingfishers. Black-crowned Night Heron, rails, and bitterns are seen or heard in the wetlands off Isaac Lake Road. The Rankin River is crossed by County Road 13 (Jenny Street) west of its intersection with Berford Street at the north end of Wiarton.

9 Oliphant and Red Bay
Shorebirds such as Wilson's Snipe, yellowlegs, Least Sandpiper, and Semipalmated Plover use the coastal mudflats, seen from shoreline roads. Offshore are the Fishing Islands, nesting grounds for Common Terns, Caspian Terns, Ring-billed and Herring Gulls, and Double-crested Cormorant.

10 Owen Sound
Inglis Falls (south of Owen Sound, on Inglis Falls Road, off Grey County Road 18), Hibou (just northeast of Owen Sound on County Road 15), and Ainslie Woods (just north of Leith) conservation areas include mature mixed forest with typical woodland birds, among them nuthatches, Eastern Phoebe, Black-and-white Warbler, and Hairy and Pileated Woodpecker. The bay itself is used by waterfowl, loons, and grebes.

Port Elgin
11 Southampton – Miramichi Bay
Offshore lies Chantry Island, a migratory bird sanctuary with nesting cormorants, herons, Great Egrets, gulls, terns, and Bald Eagles. Miramichi Bay is one of the best shorebird sites along Lake Huron. Watch for Ruddy Turnstone, Dunlin, Sanderling, and all types of waders in the spring and mid-fall.

12 MacGregor Point Provincial Park
Home to the Huron Fringe Birding Festival, there is great birding in the campground where Veery, American Redstart, and Black-throated Green Warbler are common. The wetlands at the south end are rich in birds species including Blue-gray Gnatcatcher, Blue-winged Warbler, Least Bittern, Sora, and Wood Duck. Five kilometres south of Port Elgin, off Highway 21.

Kincardine
13 Point Clark
Point Clark projects into Lake Huron, allowing viewing opportunities in the fall for migrating waterfowl, loons, gulls, and species that otherwise avoid land, known by birders as "pelagics."

Goderich
14 Hullett Provincial Wildlife Management Area
This large system of dyked

wetlands and associated forest northeast of Clinton (main parking lot is off Summerhill Road west of Kinburn) provides fine spring opportunities, with few other visitors, to observe waterfowl, harriers, rails, bitterns, and even land birds such as Northern Waterthrush and Veery.

15 Greenock Swamp Wetland Complex

This large forested wetland between Walkerton and Kincardine, north of Highway 9, is a good location to observe Wood Duck and many land birds such as Veery, Common Yellowthroat, and Northern Waterthrush.

Orangeville

16 Luther Marsh Wildlife Management Area

This vast wetland complex has many species of nesting waterfowl, bitterns, herons, one of the largest colony of breeding Great Egrets in Ontario, Northern Harrier, American Woodcock, and Wilson's Snipe. The surrounding habitats attract northern species to breed, such as Nashville Warbler and Lincoln's Sparrow. Main parking lot is off Sideroad 21 and 22, south of Monticello.

Barrie

17 Minesing Swamp

This wetland is accessible by road or, even better, by canoe. Blue-gray Gnatcatcher, Veery, Wood Duck, Wilson's Snipe, Marsh Wren, and bitterns are among the more than a hundred species you could encounter here. The wetlands conservation area is north of Angus and Essa, and south of Minesing.

18 Holland Marsh Provincial Wildlife Area

The Holland Marsh includes extensive wetland habitat where Yellow Warbler, Common Yellowthroat, Savannah Sparrow, Northern Harrier, rails, and Wilson's Snipe can be found. There is board-walked access to the wetlands. Four kilometres north of Bradford on Yonge Street, turn east on Concession 11. After three kilometres, the road turns 90 degrees north and becomes Sideroad 20. Watch for the sign on the east side.

Midland

19 Wye Marsh Provincial Wildlife Area*

Along with the visitor's centre, the interpretive trails give information about the wetlands and forests they access. Wetlands have breeding Black Tern, American and Least Bittern, Pied-billed Grebe, rails, Common Moorhen, and American Coot. The site is best known for rearing Trumpeter Swans for reintroduction into the wild; these swans have now established themselves across much of Ontario. 16160 Highway 12 East, east from Midland.

 Tiny Marsh Provincial Wildlife Area*

Several wetland compounds with varying amounts of vegetation attract water birds, including Pied-billed Grebe, ducks, geese, bitterns, herons, rails, and Black Tern. The viewing is good along dykes and from an observation tower. From Elmvale, north three kilometres to the Tiny-Floss Townline, then west four kilometres. Entrance is on the right.

 Matchedash Bay Provincial Wildlife Area

This bay contains extensive wetlands, with the full complement of wetland species including Least Bitterns and Black Terns. Adjacent forest is rich in land birds that include Yellow-throated Vireo, Golden-winged Warbler, and American Restart. Just north of Coldwater.

Orillia

 Carden Plain*

The cattle ranches and limestone plains provide savannah-like landscape teeming with grassland and scrubland species, many of which are declining in Canada, including breeding Eastern Meadowlark, Upland Sandpiper, Brown Thrasher, Grasshopper, Field and Vesper Sparrows, and Loggerhead Shrike. North of Kirkfield five kilometres, right on McNamee Road, then immediate left onto Wylie Road. Nine kilometres north on Wylie over the plain to Alvar Road. Alvar Road crosses the plain to the west.

Southern Ontario & Greater Toronto Area

Birding hot spots selected by Ted Cheskey

① Long Point
South Walsingham – Backus Woods – St. Williams Forestry Station*

This is one of the largest forest complexes in southern Ontario, and home to numerous warblers, flycatchers, the Scarlet Tanager, thrushes, and raptors. Many rare species, such as Hooded Warbler, are common in places.

② Port Rowan

Visit the Bird Studies Canada (BSC) Headquarters' wetland and trail overlooking Long Point Bay for shorebirds, waterfowl, land birds, and raptors such as Bald Eagle. The headquarters are at 115 Front Road. Check out what BSC is doing to monitor and study birds in Canada and abroad at www.bse-eoc.org.

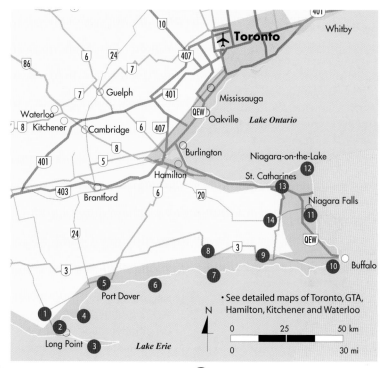

3 **Long Point***

The Long Point Peninsula stretches thirty kilometres due east, forming a large bay to the north. The causeway and marshes include parts of a National Wildlife Area. Long Point Road leads east to Long Point Provincial Park. The entire area is spectacular for land birds and water birds alike. Watch for Purple Martins and Red-headed Woodpeckers in the park and Bald Eagles and Northern Harrier over the marshes. The Long Point Bird Observatory, the oldest bird observatory in North America, operates a migration monitoring station with a small gift shop on Old Cut Boulevard near the provincial park entrance.

4 **Turkey Point***

Turkey Point Provincial Park is rich old-oak savannah forest, with land birds such as Wood Thrush, Eastern Towhee, Eastern Bluebird, Great Crested Flycatcher, and Rose-breasted Grosbeak being common. Listen at night for Whip-poor-wills. Turkey Point Road (County Road 10) runs south from Highway 24.

5 **Port Dover**

The Port Dover harbour has good food and good birding. Terns, gulls, loons, grebes, and ducks are seen in the harbour and off the lookout points to the west of the town. Watch for agile Bonaparte's Gulls and the rare Little Gull in spring and fall.

6 **Selkirk Provincial Park**
This park boasts a bird
banding station, oak
woodland, and shoreline that
attracts land birds and water
birds. Southerners such as
Carolina Wren mingle with
northern migrants in the
spring and fall. Northern Saw-
whet Owls overwinter in the
park. West side of Wheeler
Road, off Rainham Road two
kilometres west of Selkirk.

7 **Rock Point Provincial Park**
Spring and fall, this is one
of the best locations along
Lake Erie to see shorebirds.
Check the shoreline for
Yellowlegs, Sanderlings,
Ruddy Turnstones, Pectoral
Sandpipers, Semipalmated
Sandpipers, Black-bellied
Plovers, and more. East of
Port Maitland on Rymer Road,
south on Downey Road.

8 **Dunnville**
Marshes extend from
Dunnville almost to the mouth
of the Grand River. Herons,
egrets, bitterns, rails, coots,
Common Moorhens, Marsh
Wrens, terns, and swallows
can be observed spring,
summer, and fall.

9 **Wainfleet Bog**
Despite drainage and peat
extraction, this expansive
wetland is a fine birding
location where Northern
Harriers, Whip-poor-wills,
Wilson's Snipes, and a mix of
other northern and southern
species breed. Two kilometres
west of Port Colborne, take Erie
Peat Road north off Highway 3.

10 **Fort Erie***
Waterfowl congregate in the
mouth of the Niagara River
in the late fall and winter.
Watch the daily movements
of gulls and ducks, among
them Canvasbacks, Redheads,
Common Goldeneyes, and
Buffleheads. This is a good
place to observe rarities such
as King Eider.

11 **Niagara Falls***
Plan a visit in the fall and
behold thousands of gulls.
Some birders observe a dozen
species in a day, Bonaparte's
Gull, which breed in the
northern boreal forest, being
perhaps the most numerous.
Check the river for diving
ducks and loons.

12 **Niagara-on-the-Lake**
The Niagara River (the
entire river is designated
an Important Birding Area)
empties into Lake Ontario
at Niagara-on-the-Lake.
Fall birding is good, with
movements of gulls along the
shoreline (especially late in the
day) and land birds, such as
Carolina Wren and Northern
Mockingbird, as possibilities.

13 **St. Catharines**
Port Weller, the Lake Ontario
entry to the Welland Canal,

has a two-kilometre-long weir with woods and openings that are attractive for migrants. There are also good opportunities to see waterfowl and water birds.

14 Upper Twelve Mile Creek
The rich woodlands and ravines of Short Hills Provincial Park and St. Johns Conservation Area, between St. Catharines and Fonthill, harbour many forest-breeding birds, including Scarlet Tanager, Wood Thrush, and Hooded Warbler.

Hamilton area/Ancaster, Burlington, Oakville
Birding hot spots originally selected by Mike Street, updated by Ted Cheskey

1 Beamer Conservation Area
Every spring, an average of 14,500 hawks, eagles, falcons and vultures follow the Niagara Peninsula to reach more northern breeding territories. The Beamer Conservation Area in Grimsby is the best vantage point from which to see the birds that pass by Hamilton. Niagara Peninsula Hawkwatch observers are available daily to help identify raptors between March 1 and May 15. At Grimsby, take Queen Elizabeth Way exit 71/72 or Christie Street/Mountain Street (Regional Road 12) to the top of the escarpment, then right (west) on Ridge Road West (Regional Road 79) for 2.4 kilometres to Quarry Road. Follow the signs.

2 Borer's Falls Conservation Area/Hopkins Tract/Berry Conservation Area
This part of Dundas is managed by the Royal Botanical Gardens and features both trees and open fields, so look for warblers, thrushes, and grassland birds from spring through fall. For Borer's Falls Conservation Area and Hopkins Tract, follow Olympic Drive/York Road (Dundas) to Valley Road, parking off York Road between Valley Road and the railway tracks.

3 Beverly Swamp
The wet woodlands of the Beverly Swamp in Flamborough Township (Hamilton Conservation Authority) are home to warblers, vireos, and wrens from spring through fall. South from Valens to the 8th Concession Road, the n east to the parking area near the power lines.

4 Binbrook Conservation Area
At this Niagara Peninsula Conservation Authority facility, trees and open areas combine with Lake Niapenco to give a variety

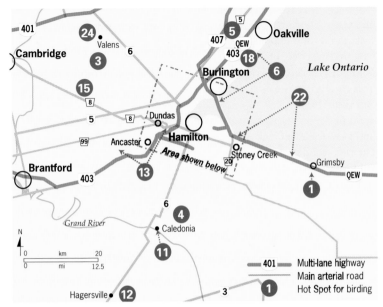

of habitats. Many grassland and forest birds, shorebirds in migration, some ducks, and the occasional raptor can be found here. Mount Hope south two kilometres on Highway 6 to Chippewa Road. Turn east and go about four kilometres, following the signs. The area is open from spring to fall. Expect to pay an entrance fee.

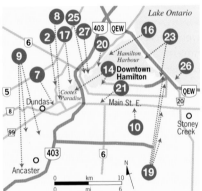

5 Bronte Provincial Park

Less than two kilometres north of the Queen Elizabeth Way on Burloak Drive, Bronte Provincial Park is an oasis for land birds during migration. Trails allow access to the heavily forested ravine, where Indigo Bunting, Gray Catbird, and Rose-breasted Grosbeak breed.

6 Burlington/Oakville Lakeshore

From late fall through mid-spring, geese, loons, grebes, and many species of ducks including scoters and Long-tailed Duck (sometimes in the tens of thousands) can be seen along this part of the west shore of Lake Ontario. Worthwhile stops include Spencer Smith Park, small lookout parks at major intersections, Sioux Lookout Park, Paletta Park (Shoreacres), the refinery pier at Burloak Road, Bronte Harbour, and Confederation Park in Oakville.

7 Desjardins Canal

This remnant of the old Dundas-Hamilton canal is a good place to look for ducks and geese, fall through spring. Off Olympic Drive east of Dundas, one hundred metres north of Cootes Drive.

8 Dundas Marsh/Cootes Paradise

The tree-lined creeks of this large area (managed by the Royal Botanical Gardens) border the marshes and lead out to a wide expanse of open water. Many bird types—herons, woodland birds, woodpeckers, shorebirds, raptors, and waterfowl—can be found, especially during spring and fall migrations. Trails start on the north side of Cootes Drive between Hamilton and Dundas: a) Hydro Pond—follow the west side of Spencer Creek past the foot bridge; b) South Shore Trail runs three kilometres from the east side of the creek at the road bridge behind McMaster to Princess Point; c) The Willows/Cootes Paradise—from the foot bridge over the creek follow the trail, keeping the creek and then the old canal close on your left past the marsh. Caution: all trails may be wet and slippery.

9 Dundas Valley Conservation Area

The rolling hills and tall trees of the Hamilton Conservation Authority's main public area attract warblers, thrushes, cuckoos, wrens, swallows, and sparrows from spring through fall, and woodpeckers and owls year-round. a) Trail Centre—off Governor's Road (Regional Road 399/99), approximately five kilometres west of Osler Drive, Dundas; b) Spring Valley/Martin Road—entrance and parking at Lion's Club Pool, off Jerseyville Road, 0.5 kilometres west of Lloyminn Avenue, Ancaster; c) Merrick Field Centre and Resource Centre, Ancaster—take Wilson Street East downhill to Montgomery Drive, then turn left to the T-intersection, right on Old Dundas Road (very steep) to the first stop sign at the bottom of the hill. Go straight ahead on Upper Lion's Club Road. Continue to the end of Upper Lion's Club for Merrick Field Centre, or turn right on Artaban Road for the Resource Centre. Expect an entrance fee.

10 Gage Park

This park's tall trees can be a haven for passerines during spring and fall migration, and owls are likely to be spotted year-round. The park is at Main Street East and Gage Avenue.

11 Grand River

South of Hamilton, around Caledonia and York, the

Grand River is home to nesting Ospreys in summer and has ducks in open water during the winter.

12 Hagersville
The open farm fields between Highway 6 and Highway 3 south of Hagersville are home to hundreds of hawks and owls in late fall and winter.

13 Hamilton-Brantford Rail Trail
Starting at Rifle Range Road in West Hamilton, this converted rail line right-of-way travels thirty kilometres west through the wooded hills and fields of the Dundas Valley into rolling farmland west of Ancaster. Possible species depend on the habitat and season. Access is at road crossings—consult maps. Parking may be limited.

14 Hamilton Harbour Waterfront Trail
Except when the harbour is iced over, gulls, swans, geese, and ducks (sometimes in the thousands) can be seen from this fully accessible paved trail, which runs from Pier 4 Park and Bayfront Park west to Princess Point and Cootes Paradise. Orioles, swallows, and warblers can also be found in spring and summer.

15 Hyde Tract
This large forest two kilometres south of Kirkwall, one kilometre east along Safari Road (Regional Road 501) from Kirkwall Road (Regional Road 52) features mostly conifers growing on a limestone base. In spring and summer, look for grouse, warblers, thrushes, and sparrows. Rails and marsh birds can be found at the swamp one kilometre further east along Safari Road, but exercise caution, as there can be heavy traffic and narrow shoulders.

16 LaSalle Park and Marina
Unless frozen over, the marina (located on the north side of Burlington Bay near Aldershot) is frequented by swans (including Trumpeter Swans from the Wye Marsh introduction program), geese, and thousands of ducks from fall to spring. Woodland birds can often be found in the adjacent park during migration.

17 Nature Centre/Arboretum/North Shore Trails
This central part of the Royal Botanical Gardens (RBG) property has different species of woodland birds depending on the season, and sometimes harbours owls and hawks. Off York Boulevard northwest of downtown Hamilton, on Old Guelph Road. Expect an entrance fee at some times of the year.

18 Paletta, McNichol, and Shoreacres parks
Between Walker's Line and

Appleby Line, off Lakeshore Road in Burlington. Good views of Lake Ontario. From October to April watch for Bufflehead, Goldeneye, other waterfowl, as well as wrens, woodpeckers, and migrants during migration.

19 Red Hill Creek Valley

More than 150 species of birds have been recorded in the Red Hill Valley. This migration corridor offers something to see regardless of the season. Habitat varies from deciduous trees along the creek at the north end to large conifers at the south end, with some fields and a golf course along the way. Access: a) Red Hill Creek mouth—east end of Eastport Drive; b) Red Hill Marsh and lower creek— Brampton Street (at the water purification plant); c) Central Valley—Red Hill Bowl parking lot (King Street and Lawrence Road); d) lower King's Forest and upper creek—Rosedale Arena (Greenhill Avenue and Rosseau Road); e) central/ upper King's Forest—Mt. Albion Road, and Mud Street near Albion Falls.

20 Royal Botanical Gardens

The headquarters of the world-renowned Royal Botanical Gardens provides access to major gardens, the Hendrie Valley and Grindstone Creek. Warblers and other passerines, herons, rails, and other marsh birds can be seen depending on the season. The gardens headquarters are at 680 Plains Road West in Burlington.

21 Sheraton Hamilton Hotel

Since 1995, the Sheraton Hamilton has been home to a very successful Peregrine Falcon nest. Most activity takes place from late May into July, but the adult birds can be seen year-round. The hotel is at 116 King Street West, near Bay Street North.

22 Stoney Creek Lakeshore Royal Botanical Gardens

From late fall through mid-spring, geese, loons, grebes, and many species of ducks (sometimes in the tens of thousands) can be seen along the south shore of Lake Ontario. Exit 88 (Centennial Parkway) or 78 (Fifty Road) to North Service Road. There are a number of lakefront accesses between Grays Road and Fifty Road. Fifty Point Conservation Area headquarters is at 1479 Baseline Road, just east of Fifty Road.

23 Tollgate Ponds/Windermere Basin

These two large ponds are home to ducks year-round, cormorants, gulls and terns, and Black-crowned Night Heron in summer, and shorebirds on the edges during migration. Tollgate Ponds: Eastport Drive, south of the lift bridge, on the west side, opposite the industrial sector. Windermere Basin: two kilometres farther on, south of Pier 24 Access Road (parking restrictions on weekdays).

 Valens Conservation Area
This park contains a large lake and wetland, as well as a good variety of habitats. A boardwalk and extensive trail system provide views of marsh habitat and opportunities to see a diversity of marsh species. Strong concentrations of waterfowl can occur on the lake in the late fall and early spring. Owned by the Hamilton Conservation Authority, this area requires a small entry fee. Just west of Valens on Regional Road 97.

 Valley Inn
Also managed by the Royal Botanical Gardens, the outlet of Grindstone Creek into the harbour here attracts gulls and terns, as well as herons and ducks from spring to fall. You can also see shorebirds, sparrows, warblers, and often Bald Eagles and Ospreys during migration. Off York Boulevard northwest of downtown Hamilton, Valley Inn Road goes east and down to the water level.

 Van Wagner's Beach and Ponds
From September to December, birders gather here to look for rare gulls, and migrating waterfowl on the beach. From spring through fall, herons and shorebirds can be found around and on the ponds, as well as sparrows and warblers in the vegetation. From QEW Exits 90 Woodward Avenue, take Beach Blvd to Van Wagner's Beach Road (follow signs for Confederation park), or QEW Exit 88 to Centennial Parkway (Hwy. 20, Stoney Creek) to Van Wagner's Beach Rd., then west (toward Skyway Bridge). The park is near Hutch's Restaurant. *Note: In 2001, all municipalities in the Hamilton-Wentworth region were amalgamated into the City of Hamilton. Former town names are given here because they are still used on maps and signs as well as by residents.*

 Woodland Cemetery
The cemetery's location on a peninsula jutting into Hamilton Harbour makes it both a migrant trap and a migration path. Warblers and vireos feed in the trees in spring and fall. On some days during fall migration, thousands of small birds—30 to 40 species—as well as hawks and eagles, can be seen overhead in a single day. Check the trees at the harbour edges for Bald Eagles and Ospreys, especially in fall. Follow Spring Gardens Road westbound behind the Royal Botanical Gardens'

headquarters. Drive past the buildings into the cemetery, then bear left (south) toward Hamilton Harbour.

Kitchener-Waterloo, Cambridge, Guelph
Birding hot spots selected by Ted Cheskey

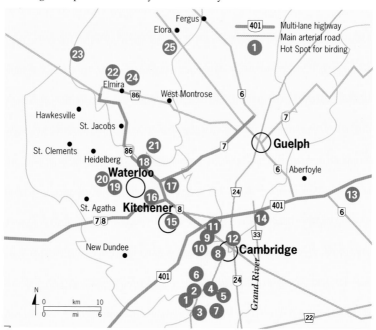

1 **Dickson Wilderness Area**
This small natural area has a leisurely half-hour loop trail that links to Wrigley and Bannister Lakes. Very tame Black-capped Chickadees are present in all seasons so bring sunflower seeds. There is a small wetland and some upland oak-maple forest, as well as conifers and remnant prairie. This is a good place for winter birding. The area is owned by the Grand River Conservation Authority (GRCA). Four kilometres west of Glen Morris along Glen Morris / Brant-Waterloo Road (Regional Road 28) to Spragues Road (Regional Road 75). The parking lot is about one kilometre from the intersection, just after the "S" bend on the north side.

2 **Bannister and Wrigley Lakes**
These two natural lakes are worth checking for waterbirds and shorebirds during spring and fall migrations. A tower on Bannister Lake (north side) and parking lot provide good access and views. Good numbers of waterfowl, including Ring-necked Duck, are present in April. Herons and other large

waders can be seen feeding along the northeastern part of the lake in early spring, summer and fall. The lakes are owned by the Grand River Conservation Authority (GRCA) and are located just west of Spragues Road (Regional Road 75) on Wrigley Road (Regional Road 49).

3 **Pinehurst Conservation Area**

To enter this conservation area, you must pay a small daily fee (which will also give you access to all GRCA sites). Pinehurst also has camping. The forest around Pinehurst has plentiful oak, hickory, and pine. The great diversity of forest-breeding birds in the area includes several warbler and vireo species, Red-bellied Woodpecker, and perhaps Indigo Bunting and Eastern Towhee in the rolling fields on the east side of the park. Pinehurst is eight kilometres north of Paris on Pinehurst Road.

4 **Sudden Tract**

This large tract of rich interior deciduous and mixed forest has many trails, including a 700-metre boardwalk traversing a large swamp wetland. This is a good place to see Pileated and Red-bellied Woodpeckers, but is great for birding in all seasons. The Sudden Tract parking lot is about a five-minute drive south of Cambridge on the

east side of Spragues Road between Greenfield Road and Beke Road. There is also access off Beke Road along the south side of the forest.

5 **Grass Lake or Cranberry Bog**

This wetland has both marsh and bog habitats. A good range of breeding marsh species are found here, including Sora and Virginia Rail. The antenna fields to the east are good for Savannah and other grassland sparrows. In winter, check for Rough-legged Hawks and other birds of prey. Turn east onto Beke Road off Spragues Road, drive about two kilometres, take the first right (Shouldice Side Road), then watch for wetlands on the east side of the road. Birding is from the roadside.

6 **Alps Hills**

This large deciduous forest is home to many forest interior breeding birds and area-sensitive scrubland species. Following the Grand Valley Trail south from the parking lot, you eventually come to a nice view over mixed farmland. This lookout is a good area for Eastern Towhee and Brown Thrasher, as well as for observing raptors. Alps Hills is owned both by the Grand River Conservation Authority (GRCA) and privately. The parking lot is on the south side of Alps Road between Shouldice Side

Road (Regional Road 71) and Dumfries Road 47.

7 Cambridge to Paris Rail Trail

This rail trail runs along the east side of the river from Cambridge to Paris. There are several access points where you can leave your car. Best access is off Washington Street in Glen Morris. Hiking south, you pass through a variety of habitats and approach the river in several places. Many interesting birds breed along the river bottom of the forest, including Blue-winged and Chestnut-sided Warblers and Least Flycatcher. North of Glen Morris on the west side of the river, cedar seepage provides breeding habitat to White-throated Sparrows. During winter months, Bald Eagles are frequently observed along the river. Cliff Swallows nest beneath the bridge. The area is under both public and private ownership.

8 Victoria Park, Mountview Cemetery

In the winter, both the city park and the adjacent cemetery can be good locations for winter finches as well as hard-to-find winter species such as the Red-breasted Nuthatch and Brown Creeper. During migration, this area is worth checking for flocks of warblers and thrushes. The park and cemetery are located in the City of Cambridge, with access

off Salisbury, Wentworth, and Blenheim Roads.

9 Riverbank Trail – Linear Trail Section

This linear city park follows the Speed River to its confluence with the Grand, then continues several hundred metres downstream. Pockets of trees and shrubs along the river can be great migrant traps, particularly in May and prior to rain. Bald Eagles and other birds of prey, as well as an impressive list of waterfowl and landbirds, have been observed from this park. The trail is owned by the City of Cambridge. Access and parking are off Bishop and Hamilton streets, and Riverside Drive and Rose Street.

10 Walter Bean Trail – Grand Trunk Section

A trail runs parallel to the Grand River through forest, old field, and riparian habitats. This trail is part of the Walter Bean Trail, or Grand River Trail—a system of trails adjacent to the Grand River that traverse the region of Waterloo from end to end. On this section, side trails to the river add to the habitat diversity. This area, including the river, offers excellent all-season birding, with a good variety of breeders and perhaps the greatest variety of winter birds of any single area within the region. Great

Black-backed Gull, American Wigeon, and Gadwall can be seen on the river in the winter. The area also acts as a migrant trap. The trail is owned both publicly and privately. Access is off Blair Road (roadside parking) and George Street (parking lot).

⑪ Riverside Park

This park boasts good wetland habitat and open marsh. Trails into the adjacent forest are good for migrant landbirds and for winter birding. Look especially for marsh species in wintertime. The park is also known for its tame chickadees, which people hand feed. The park is owned by the City of Cambridge. 49 King Street West (in Preston).

⑫ Shades Mills

This area includes a fairly large reservoir and many kilometres of trails through a wide variety of habitats. It is good for breeding, migrant, and winter birds. Keep an eye out for Indigo Bunting and Baltimore Oriole. There is a small fee for entry. Shades Mills is owned by the Grand River Conservation Authority. 450 Avenue Road, Cambridge.

⑬ Mountsberg Conservation Area

This large reservoir and wetland has excellent spring, summer, and fall birding. It is home to nesting Ospreys in the summer and to visiting shorebirds and ducks in spring and fall. Pied-billed Grebes, Green Herons, and numerous other water birds are observed here, and Turkey Vultures are never far away. The Birds of Prey Centre is worth a visit. The conservation area entrance is off Milburough Line, one kilometre north of the intersection with Campbellville Road. Expect an entrance fee.

⑭ Puslinch Lake

This is the largest natural lake within the region. Excellent views of the lake can be had from the north; canoes are rented out for a small fee. Presently, there is no public or private access to the south shore. Puslinch Lake can have some of the best regional concentrations of waterfowl and other waterbirds, including loons and ducks in the early spring and late fall to early winter. Many power boats are out on the lake from late spring to fall. Exit Highway 401 at Townline Road and turn east almost immediately on Regional Road No. 32. The only access is at McClintock's, a private marina and restaurant on the right, about one kilometre from the turnoff.

⑮ Homer Watson Park

Trails head off in all directions here. Take the trail to the left to go onto a bluff overlooking the Grand River. This is a good place for migrant landbirds and winter birds. Trails through the park can also be productive for landbirds. In April, this is a good place to view all species of swallows. Highway 8 north five kilometres from Highway 401 across the Grand River. Turn southwest onto Fairway Road for one kilometre to Wilson Avenue. Turn left onto Wilson and follow it to the end (it's a dead-end road).

16 Lakeside Park

This small urban park includes a natural lake, wetland, and a mix of natural and manicured habitats. Birding can be good during migration (look for thrushes, warblers, and sparrows in late April through May) and in the winter. Off the Conestoga Parkway (Highway 7) onto Homer Watson Road North. Follow to the end (one kilometre) and turn left onto Stirling and Greenbrook. The park will be just in front of you.

17 Highway 7 Walter Bean Trail – Grand River Trail

The riparian habitat and scrub here provide excellent feeding areas for migrating land birds. Watch the river for all species of swallows, Kingfisher, and Great Blue Heron. The trail follows the river into Bingeman's Park. Take Victoria Street east toward Breslau. Parking and access is to the left (north side of the road) just west of the bridge over the Grand River.

18 Bechtel Park

The forest, lowland meadow, and scrub habitats are accessible from the soccer fields. During migration, land birds can be especially good, although these areas are worth checking in all seasons. Take the Conestoga Parkway (Highway 85) north into Waterloo. Exit onto University Avenue East. Turn right onto Bridge Street and right again into the park.

19 Columbia Lake and Forest

The trail here crosses old fields and some small woodlands. It is very popular with walkers. (Development is occurring to the east.) The small forests along Laurel Creek can be very good for landbirds in winter. Where the creek empties into Columbia Lake, mudflats (in spring and fall) can be productive for shorebirds. Check the reservoir for ducks and unusual gulls in the fall. These can also be viewed from Columbia Street. Exit the Parkway (Highway 85) west onto Northfield Drive West. Northfield becomes Westmount Road. Turn right onto Bearinger Road and immediately right into the parking lot. Trails start across

the road (south side). Take
the trail on the east side of
Laurel Creek, going south from
Bearinger.

20 Laurel Lake Conservation Area

Laurel Lake can be excellent
for waterfowl and gulls in the
fall to early winter before the
water is drained, as well as in
the early to mid-spring. Least
Bitterns have been sighted
in the marshes on the west
side of the road. Soras and
Virginia Rails have also been
spotted here. After turning
right onto Bearinger Road
from Westmount Road, turn
right onto Laurelwood Drive,
then right again onto Beaver
Creek Road. Pull over along
the causeway. There are good
views of the reservoir from the
causeway and culvert/bridge.

21 Kiwanis Park, Walter Bean Trail

Beyond the huge swimming
pool, the Walter Bean Trail
follows the Grand River
through good migrant bird
habitat. Orioles are very
common here. The area is also
good for winter birds. Follow
University Avenue east from
the Parkway (Highway 85).
Cross Bridge Street and carry
on to Woolwich Street. Turn
right onto Woolwich and left
onto Kiwanis Park Drive into
the Kiwanis Park parking lot.

22 Floradale Reservoir

When water levels are drawn
down in the late summer and

fall, this reservoir provides
the best shorebird habitat in
the region and is well worth
a visit. From Elmira, four
kilometres north on Regional
Road 21 to Florapine Road.
Turn left. About one kilometre
along, to the south, is the
Floradale Reservoir.

23 Floradale Flats

The landscape here is sparsely
forested and comprises mainly
expansive, flat, and relatively
high farmland. During the
winter, this area is the best
site to observe large birds of
prey, including Rough-legged
Hawks. On occasion, other
open-country specialties such as
Rough-legged Hawk, Northern
Harrier, Snowy Owl, Snow
Bunting, Horned Lark, and
Lapland Longspur can be found
in this area. This landscape is
situated between Floradale,
Macton, and Conestogo Lake.

24 Sandy Hills

The large forest along the
road is made up of mature
conifer plantations, owned by
the Region of Waterloo. The
trails are for multiple use. This
area harbours excellent forest
interior bird habitat. Mature
plantations attract more
northern breeding species—
the Yellow-rumped Warbler,
Red-breasted Nuthatch, and
Golden-crowned Kinglet
have all bred here. About five
kilometres north of Elmira
on Regional Road 21 (Arthur

Street North), turn right onto Sandy Hills Drive.

25 Elora Conservation Area

The Elora Conservation Area is just south of the town of Elora. It is located on the Grand River, just west of Fergus (in Wellington County). The gorge and park are heavily forested with many trails that are good for migrants as well as breeding birds and several species of warblers. The entrance into the park is off Regional Road 21, on the east side of the Grand River.

Toronto/GTA

Toronto Birding hot spots originally selected by Hugh Currie, updated by Ted Cheskey

1 Rattray's Marsh

At this birding destination, you will find fairly extensive woods and a marsh with a viewing platform, allowing you to see the ducks and shorebirds. Canada Geese are often present on the lake and the woods are excellent for birds year-round. From Lakeshore Road go south on Bexhill Road (which is three kilometres west of Mississauga Road and two kilometres east of Southdown). Go 0.8 kilometres towards the lake. Near the parking lot, you will see a map of the area.

2 Marie Curtis Park

The lawns here are vast, and the park is bisected by Etobicoke Creek. Marie Curtis offers an opportunity to see waterfowl from close up at the feeding area at the river. Farther west, there is an extensive woodland, which is good for migrants. Sometimes owls can be found here as well. Much of these woods are private property, but the huge gaps in the fence and the many trails suggest that there is no problem birding here. From Dixie Road at Lakeshore Road, go 0.7 kilometres east, then turn right (south) to the park.

3 Colonel Samuel Smith Park

This landfill has been improved to add ponds and marshes, and there is a viewing platform. If you walk all the way to the end, you may find Horned Larks and other winter birds during that season. The ponds and marshes are good for ducks and rails, while the huge old spruce trees to the north are often excellent for migratory birds. Check also the old orchard to the west of the rows of spruce trees. Go south on Kipling Avenue past Lakeshore Road to the parking lot close to the lake.

4 **Humber Bay East and West Parks**
Both of these large parks have close-cut lawns, but the east portion of Humber Bay East has been allowed to grow rank. As the bushes and trees continue to mature, the birding will improve. On both of these artificially created peninsulas, waterfowl can be seen at close range, and there has been some landscaping on Humber Bay East, which attracts ducks to the shoreline. Humber Bay West offers a good view of the bay to the north. From the parking lot near the base of Humber Bay Park Road West, walk west along the boardwalk to the gazebo and beyond. In winter, many gulls can be seen from here, roosting on the yacht club docks. These parks can be reached by the Queen streetcar, or by exiting the Gardiner Expressway at Park Lawn Road and going south to the lake.

5 **High Park**
This huge park is undergoing restoration to its original vegetation. Check the marsh at the north end of Grenadier Pond for rails, then the pond itself. Continue up the hill, past the Grenadier Restaurant, to Colborne Lodge. Walk east from here to the duck ponds, then north along Spring Road. In the fall, join the hawk-watchers on the hill,

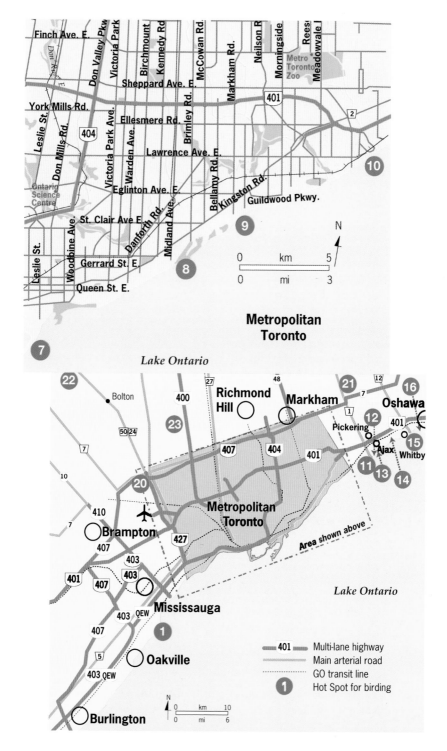

just north of the restaurant. The park is easily reached by the TTC subway. Go to High Park station, then walk south across Bloor Street. If driving, park near the north pedestrian entrance at Bloor and Parkdale, and walk west, then south along the trails, or drive to the road entrance at Bloor and Colborne Lodge Drive.

6 Toronto Islands

An entire day is needed to fully explore the islands. The best birding area is the Island Nature Sanctuary (not signposted) just north of the Island Nature School. One should also check the beaches, on the west and south sides, for shorebirds and ducks. The woods south of the Ward's Island village can be good for migrants. Ferries leave from the foot of Bay Street to Hanlan's Point, Centre Island, or Ward's Island. From mid-October to April, ferry schedules are restricted, but even at minimum winter service ferries run hourly to Ward's.

7 Tommy Thompson Park

This landfill stretches 4.8 kilometres out to a lighthouse. There are few amenities and it can be very cold in winter. There are huge colonies of Ring-billed Gulls, Double-crested Cormorants, and Black-crowned Night Herons. Spotted Sandpipers may be found along the shoreline.

In recent years, Canvasbacks have nested in a small pond two kilometres out. Nearby, Ashbridge's Bay Park can also be good. When driving from the city centre, go east on the Gardiner Expressway to Leslie Street, then turn south. A bus runs every half-hour part of the way to the park from May 24 to Thanksgiving. The best fields and marshes are at the base.

8 Bluffer's Park

This is another landfill area, which often harbours waterfowl and shorebirds on the lake or in the park's ponds. It gives a good view of the spectacular cliffs, which may hold Peregrine Falcons and Bank Swallows. At the lake end of Brimley Road South.

9 East Point Park

This is another area where thousands of truckloads of landfill have been converted into an attractive park. However, there are no wilderness areas as at Leslie Spit (Tommy Thompson Park). East Point Park has flocks of ducks in winter and attracts shorebirds around the big pond at its centre. The nearby cliffs may hold Peregrine Falcons, and raptors can be seen at times in migration. Follow Beechgrove Drive south off Lawrence Avenue East, just west of Lawrence and Meadowvale Road.

Rouge Beach Park

The Rouge River flows through here, creating a marsh and ponds along its length. There are many trails in this very large park, but the best one is at the mouth, on the east side of the river. Cliff Swallows nest under the bridge. The marsh may harbour rails and Common Yellowthroat. Parking is best on the west side of Rouge Beach. From Port Union Road and Fanfare Avenue, go east on Fanfare to East Avenue, right (south) on East Ave. a few metres to Ridgewood Road. Follow Ridgewood to where it ends at the lake.

 Frenchman's Bay

Frenchman's Bay in Pickering has extensive yacht clubs close to Lake Ontario, but the north end is still in a state of wilderness. The area can be excellent for shorebirds in August and September. You will also see waterfowl, and the small woods often hold migrants. From White's Road, 0.3 kilometres south of exit off the 401, go left (east) on Bayly Street. Go east 1.8 kilometres to a community centre on the lakeside and park here in the southeast corner. Walk east on the trail. Rubber boots are advisable.

 Hydro Park

This park has migrants in spring and fall, a marsh for shorebirds and ducks and a view of the lake at the Pickering Nuclear Station. Take Brock Road from the 401 in Pickering all the way south to Montgomery Park Road. Head west 0.8 kilometres to Sandy Beach Road, then north 0.5 kilometres to a parking lot on the west side. Walk along the trail through the woods to get to the marsh.

 Squire's Beach

Squire's Beach has vast cattail marshes bordering Duffin Creek. The river broadens into a large pond a few hundred metres before reaching Lake Ontario. This area is also good for shorebirds and even better for waterfowl, as well as Great Blue Herons and Ospreys. Check the bushes for land birds and follow the short trails to the edge of the pond to see the birdlife there. More birds can be seen by going south to the end of Frisco Road, then walking east along the bicycle path. The directions begin the same as for Hydro Park, but at Montgomery Park Road, go east 0.3 kilometres to McKay Road. Turn left (north) on McKay and follow it as it turns east and then southeast to become Jodrel Road, then to intersect Montgomery Park Road. Park near the intersection on the east side of Jodrel.

 Cranberry Marsh

Cranberry Marsh is a large

natural pond in Whitby with cattail marshes around its borders. Of all the birding areas around Toronto, this one is usually the most productive. The large pond holds waterfowl in all seasons, while the forest edges are excellent for migrants. There are two boardwalks that lead to viewing towers on the west side. In September and October, a well-organized hawk watch takes place on the south platform. Days with a few cumulus clouds and a north or northwest wind are best. Nearby Lynde Shores woodlot is a delight for children because the small birds take seeds and nuts right from the hand. From Salem Road South (exit south off the 401) and Bayly Street East, go east 2.3 kilometres to Regional Road 23 (Lake Ridge Road), where Bayly becomes Victoria Street West. After a short distance farther east, take Hall's Road on the right.

 Thickson Woods

This small oasis of forest in Oshawa was saved from destruction by fundraising efforts of birders. Migrants are concentrated here, especially in springtime. There are several trails through the woods and a sightings book. For at least two decades, Great Horned Owls have nested here, although one must spend time looking in the pines to

find them. To the east are Corbett Creek and a plentiful marsh. The semi-open area to the north has also recently been acquired by naturalists, and trails are being developed. At the lake end of Thickson Road, south of the exit from the 401. Take the second-last left and park here on the road.

 Second Marsh

There is a small lake at the centre of Second Marsh in Oshawa. On the north is an extensive woodland, with well-developed trails and a viewing tower. On the east, after parking in the General Motors (GM) parking lot, visit another viewing tower, then walk the trail down to Lake Ontario. In fall, the west side often has extensive mudflats, attracting hundreds of shorebirds. Among the many gulls are often some Great Black-backed. Ducks may include any of the species in this book. Take exit 419 (Bloor Street / Harmony Road) off Highway 401, go south on Farewell Street (Regional Road 56) 0.8 kilometres to Colonel Sam Drive, then east. Visit the woodland trail, which begins just west of the bridge, before continuing to GM.

Cedarvale Ravine

This mid-city ravine in Toronto has been adversely affected in recent years by the erection of apartment buildings. There are some cattail marsh areas and some dry pine forest, as well as numerous bird feeders, which attract winter birds behind the houses at the tops of the hills. These birds may include finches, woodpeckers, nuthatches, cardinals, and others. The ravine begins at the north entrance to the St. Clair West subway station and continues northwest. It can also be reached by driving to Bathurst Street and St. Clair Avenue, then north one block, then right (east) to the subway exit. Another ravine continues southeast on the south side of St. Clair.

18 Lambton Woods

Much of this area consists of manicured lawn, which has few birds, but the wet woods here are fairly extensive. Of the many good birding areas along the Humber River, none is better than Lambton Woods. There are ducks and gulls on the river, and landbirds, including the Red-bellied Woodpecker. Several feeders attract small birds, many of which will take seeds from the hand. Eastern Screech-Owls are common here, although difficult to find in the day. Go south from Eglinton Avenue on Scarlett Road for 0.3 kilometres to Edenbridge Drive. Turn right (west), drive for 1.1 kilometres and enter the James Gardens parking lot. Walk south from here.

19 Wilket Creek and Sunnybrook Parks

This is an area of widespread pine and deciduous forest on both sides of the Don River. Spring is the best time to visit, as the parks become congested with picnickers in summer. Belted Kingfishers can be found along the river. The woods can be good for finches, waxwings, Eastern Screech-owls, and many other species. From Eglinton Avenue East and Leslie Street, go 0.2 kilometres north on Leslie, then left into the park. The roads and trails extend for 1.5 kilometres to the north and northwest.

20 Clairville Conservation Area

This area comprises woodlands and fields, as well as a big reservoir. This area can be good for small owls and hawks in winter. Field birds like Savannah Sparrows are common. To reach the best section, go to the intersection of Highways 50 (Albion Road / Country Road 50) and 27, then west on 50. After the road has curved to the north, you will see a little gate and a road leading west. Follow this road to a creek valley surrounded by bushes and trees.

21 Claremont Conservation Area

This is an extensive woodland with a creek flowing through the centre. This is one of the few locations near Toronto where Ruffed Grouse can be seen. In winter, the whole area is good for northern finches like the Evening Grosbeak. The west border has many multiflora bushes that attract Cedar Waxwings. The conservation area is southeast of Claremont, on the 7th Concession (1.7 kilometres north of Highway 7) just west of Westney Road North. The parking lot is on the north side of the road.

 Palgrave Conservation Area

This is an excellent area for birds, especially in winter. There are fields, extensive forests, cedar bogs, and ponds. Wild Turkeys can be found here, or at feeders in winter a little farther west, especially along Centreville Creek Avenue. This is a good place to find Sharp-shinned Hawks, Black and White Warblers, Golden-crowned Kinglets, and many other birds. 16500 Highway 50 (County Road 50), eight kilometres north of Bolton and two kilometres south of Palgrave.

 Kortright Centre for Conservation

This area holds open fields and woods. Staff members lead guided nature walks, including "owl prowls." The diverse flora north of the buildings is good for American Robins, Northern Cardinals, and Gray Catbirds. There is a daily entrance fee. For information, call (416) 667-6299. 9550 Pine Valley Drive, in Vaughan, between Major MacKenzie Drive West and Rutherford Road.

 Humber Arboretum

The woodlands and fields are immediately west of Humber College. They can be good for migrants in spring and fall and owls in winter. At Highway 27 and Humber College Boulevard (just south of Finch Avenue West), go left (west), enter the huge parking area and head for the southwest corner, where the arboretum is located. The trails begin here.

Southeastern and Eastern Ontario

Toronto Birding hot spots selected by Ted Cheskey

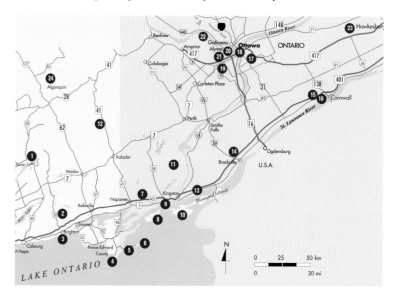

① Stony Lake
Petroglyph Provincial Park
Look for woodpeckers, White-winged Crossbill, and Evening Grosbeak in the park's bogs and pine forests, among other northerly species. Watch for Bald and Golden Eagles scavenging deer carcasses in winter months. 2249 Northey's Bay Road, south, then east from Woodview, and just northeast of Stoney Ridge.

② Brighton
Murray Marsh Natural Habitat Area
South of Percy Reach on the Trent River is this large swamp wetland. Breeding rails, bitterns, and Wood Ducks are present in marshy areas and Northern Waterthrush, Common Yellowthroat, and Veery can be spotted or heard in the forest. North of Codrington, follow Goodfellow Road east off Regional Road 30.

③ Presqu'ile Provincial Park*
Perhaps the best all-round birding location in Ontario, Presqu'ile's combination of deep forest, open forest, meadow, marsh, mudflats, beach, and rocky shoals attracts all types of birds. Shorebirds such as Short-billed Dowitcher, Sanderling, and Dunlin are best viewed in May and from August to October. A huge colony of cormorants, gulls, and herons breed on Gull and High Bluff islands. Waterfowl of all

types appear in the bay or on the lake. Land-bird viewing during breeding season, and especially in spring migration, can be spectacular. 328 Presqu'ile Parkway, Brighton

④ Prince Edward County
Point Petre Provincial Wildlife Area*

This site offers very good remote birding during migration. Watch for White-winged Scoter, Long-tailed Duck, Bufflehead, mergansers, and other ducks on the lake. Southwest corner of Prince Edward County, along Army Reserve Road.

⑤ Ostrander Point Crown Land Block

Excellent location for observing large numbers of spring and fall migrants. The stunted trees, patchy marsh and grassy fields are home in the spring and summer to many breeding scrubland species such as Brown Thrasher, Eastern Kingbird and cuckoo species. In the fall this can be an impressive place to observe migrating hawks. Take Ostrander Point Road toward the lake.

⑥ Prince Edward Point National Wildlife Area*

A superb location with forest, meadows, and a banding station, PEP is both a migrant trap, excellent for spotting migrating land birds, and a place with superb views of Lake Ontario for observing migrating loons, birds of prey, grebes, and ducks. A bird observatory operates in the National Wildlife Area, and is renowned for the large numbers of Saw-whet Owls that are trapped and banded there in the fall. Take Long Point Road to the eastern tip of the county.

⑦ Napanee
Napanee Barrens*

Explore the roads north and east of Napanee where the barren landscape attracts uncommon scrubland-breeding species such as cuckoos, thrashers, towhees, bluebirds, and the very rare Loggerhead Shrike.

⑧
Amherst Island*

Bundle up and explore Amherst Island in the winter, when birds of prey concentrate here. Watch for Short-eared Owls, Snowy Owls, Snow Buntings and Lapland Longspurs in fields, and Northern Saw-whet Owls in the accessible cedar woodlots. Dress warmly in the winter!

⑨ Kingston
Accessible Lemoine Point Conservation Area

Accessible Lemoine Point Conservation Area is a good place to see many water birds such as cormorants, Long-tailed Ducks, Scaups, Redheads, Canvasbacks, gulls, and terns. West of the Kingston Airport, the conservation area has two entrances: off Coverdale Road at the north, and off Front Road at the south.

Wolfe Island

Wolfe Island is much like Amherst Island, with barren farmland, woodlots, and, depending on the year and season, many owls and hawks feeding on cyclically abundant voles. A large and controversial wind energy farm was built on the west side of the island in 2009.

Frontenac Provincial Park

This park provides opportunities to observe classic Canadian Shield species such as Common Loon, Great Blue Heron, Belted Kingfisher and Osprey, and a great variety of land birds from Yellow-bellied Sapsuckers to Ruffed Grouse. 1090 Salmon Lake Road. From Sydenham on Frontenac County Road 9 go north thirteen kilometres on County Road 19 to Salmon Lake Road. Drive 2.9 kilometres to the Park.

Bon Echo Provincial Park

Bon Echo attracts northerly species such as Swainson's Thrush, Evening Grosbeaks, and crossbills. Also watch for Pileated Woodpecker, Red-breasted Nuthatch, Broad-winged Hawk, and a great

variety of other land birds. Listen for Barred Owls at night. North of Kaladar on Highway 41, and north of Cloyne.

Ivey Lea – Thousand Islands National Park

The St. Lawrence River at the community of Ivy Lea is an excellent place to observe gulls, including the Greater Black-backed, and ducks, such as the Common Goldeneye, as well as Bald Eagles and other land birds.

Brockville

North of Brockville is Mac Johnson Wildlife Area. A large forest, wetland, and reservoir provide good birding opportunities. Four kilometres north of Brockville to Tincap, then east on Debruge Road.

Cornwall

Upper Canada National Migratory Bird Sanctuary

This sanctuary, east of Morrisburg, has well-planned trails with viewing blinds that lead through a variety of habitats, from meadows to ponds. Canada and Snow Geese, Mallard, American Black Duck, Northern Pintails and other waterfowl can be viewed, depending on the season. West of Cornwall on County Road 2, about 3.5 kilometres east of Upper Canada Village.

16 Long Sault Parkway
The Long Sault Parkway offers good views of the St. Lawrence River. Watch for Great Black-backed, Iceland and Glaucous Gulls among the Herring and Ring-billed Gulls at the Saunders Dam and Power Station in winter. The Parkway loops south of County Road 2 between Ingleside and Long Sault.

17 Mer Bleue Conservation Area
Just east of Ottawa, Mer Bleue is a large forest with expansive peat bog. Many interesting northern species have nested here, including Lincoln's Sparrow and Sedge Wren, and Nashville, Yellow-rumped, and even Palm Warbler. Anderson Road runs through the Area.

Ottawa

18 Ottawa River trails – National Capital Commission
The NCC has a superb trail system and green belt the runs dozens of kilometres along the Ontario side and the Quebec side of the Ottawa River, providing access by bicycle and foot to the river and its habitats. East of the Deschenes rapids, the area around the Champlain bridge including Bate's Island is good for water fowl, especially in the fall and winter. East of Ottawa past Orléans are the Petrie Islands, which have a nature reserve and trail through marsh and wetlands.

19 Sarsaparilla, Stony Swamp and Jack Pine Trails
These conservation lands in the southwest of the city have good winter birding along the trails through mixed and coniferous forest. Watch for finches, chickadees, nuthatches, and sparrows such as White-throated.

20 Britannia Conservation Area
Mud Lake, pine forest, deciduous woodland, and edge habitats in an urban setting on the city's west side combine to make a tremendous migrant trap. The Deschênes Rapids attracts large numbers of gull and waterfowl, such as Common Goldeneye and Bufflehead, and occasionally Harlequin Duck in the winter. East on Cassels Street 0.4 kilometres from the intersection with Britannia Road.

21 Shirley's Bay
Shirley's Bay is just west of the city. Access off Rifle Road, a small NCC parking lot is the departure place to access Shirley's Bay. This land is owned by the Department of National Defense (DND) and is used occasionally for target practice. Clearance from the DND is required for access. The wetlands back of the dyke that projects into the Ottawa River are excellent for viewing waterfowl, waterbirds, and shorebirds.

Constance Bay

This bay in the Ottawa River, between Arnprior and Ottawa, is an excellent birding location year-round. Check for waterfowl, terns, shorebirds, land birds and hawks. Constance Bay Road runs east off Dunrobin Road (Regional Road 9) north of Woodlawn.

 Alfred Bog

About six kilometres south of Alfred and just north of Fenaghvale is the expansive Alfred Bog. Sandhill Cranes and Lincoln's Sparrows can be seen or heard along the boardwalk, and Short-eared Owls have nested in the bog.

Algonquin Provincial Park

Birding hot spots selected by Ron Tozer

Park visitors can get a free Algonquin Information Guide at the gates when they purchase their permit. This provides complete information about the Park and includes a map of the Highway 60 Corridor with all locations in this section shown, plus a map showing access to Barron Canyon Road and the East Side areas described here.

Highway 60 Corridor:

Birding sites described below can be located using kilometre markers along Highway 60 from km 0 at the West Gate to km 56 just past the East Gate.

Western Uplands Backpacking Trail

This trail starts at km 3 on Highway 60. Check the coniferous forest bordering the entrance area and the first half-kilometre of this trail for Black-backed Woodpecker, Boreal Chickadee, Winter Wren, and Northern Parula. Listen at night from March to May along the Oxtongue River valley near here for calling Northern Saw-whet Owls.

Whiskey Rapids Trail

Located at km 7.2 on Highway 60, much of this trail runs along the Oxtongue River through coniferous forest. Look for Spruce Grouse, Black-backed Woodpecker, Boreal Chickadee, Brown Creeper, and warblers such as Northern Parula, Magnolia, Black-and-white, American Redstart, Ovenbird, Northern Waterthrush, and Canada. The trail length is 2.1 kilometres.

Tea Lake Dam Picnic Area

Located at km 8.1 on Highway 60. Check the open water of the Oxtongue River below the dam for early migrant ducks in March and April when ponds and lakes are still frozen. Black-backed Woodpeckers are

often seen on the utility poles
along the highway here.

Hardwood Lookout Trail
This trail through hardwood
forest is at km 13.8 on
Highway 60. It is 1 kilometre
in length and features
such birds as Yellow-
bellied Sapsucker, Pileated
Woodpecker, Eastern Wood-
Pewee, Least Flycatcher, Wood
Thrush, and Scarlet Tanager.
After dark, try vocal imitations
or recordings to get a response
from Barred Owls, here and
elsewhere in nearby hardwood
forest.

Mizzy Lake Trail
This 10.8-kilometre loop trail
starts at km 15.4 on Highway
60. It visits nine small lakes
and ponds, which provide
excellent chances of seeing
moose, beaver, and birds. The
Wolf Howl Pond and West
Rose Lake sections are good
for Wood Duck, Ring-necked
Duck, Hooded Merganser,
Spruce Grouse, American
Bittern, Wilson's Snipe,
Black-backed Woodpecker,
Olive-sided Flycatcher,
Yellow-bellied Flycatcher,
Alder Flycatcher, Boreal
Chickadee, Winter Wren, and
Lincoln's Sparrow. Birders
can access this part of the trail
by driving 4.8 kilometres up
the Arowhon Road from the
trail entrance, turning right
onto an abandoned railway
and driving 0.6 kilometres to a

chain gate. Park there without
blocking access through
the locked gate and walk
eastward on the railway for 1.5
kilometres to Wolf Howl Pond
and then another kilometre
to West Rose Lake. Continue
another 0.5 kilometres to reach
"Flycatcher Bog," which often
has Olive-sided Flycatcher,
Yellow-bellied Flycatcher, and
Alder Flycatcher.

Bat Lake Trail
This trail is at km 30 on
Highway 60. It passes through
mixed poplar-birch-spruce-
fir forest that can be good for
Spruce Grouse, Black-backed
Woodpecker, Gray Jay, Boreal
Chickadee, Winter Wren,
Golden-crowned Kinglet, and
various warblers. The trail is
5.8 kilometres in length.

Old Airfield
This site is reached by taking
the Mew Lake Campground
access road at km 30.6 on
Highway 60. Follow it past
the campground office and
woodyard to a parking lot
on the left bordering the old
airfield. This large open field
with its shrubby borders
provides suitable breeding
habitat for Savannah Sparrow
and Lincoln's Sparrow.
Regular migrants found
here include American
Kestrel, Merlin, Horned Lark,
American Pipit, Le Conte's
Sparrow, Lapland Longspur,
Snow Bunting, and Eastern

Meadowlark. The airfield and its borders should be thoroughly searched on foot since it has produced many rarities over the years.

Two Rivers Trail

Located at km 31 on Highway 60, this trail goes 2.3 kilometres through mixed forest that may contain Black-backed Woodpecker, Gray Jay, Boreal Chickadee, Golden-crowned Kinglet, and warblers such as Nashville, Magnolia, Yellow-rumped, Black-and-white, and American Redstart.

Lake of Two Rivers Campground

This campground is at km 31.8 on Highway 60 and features mixed pine and white birch forest. It may have Merlin, Ruffed Grouse, Brown Creeper, Blue-headed Vireo, and Pine Warbler. At dawn during spring and fall, try the swimming beach for shorebirds, and survey the lake for migrant waterfowl such as scaup, Long-tailed Duck, Common Goldeneye, and scoters.

Trailer Sanitation Station

Enter this site at km 35.6 on Highway 60 and park in the lot to the left, just before the RV facilities. Walk a short distance past the closed gate on the Blackfox Lake portage road to view an old beaver pond adjacent to the gravel pit. Birds at the pond often include American Bittern, Great Blue Heron, Wood Duck, Hooded Merganser, Olive-sided Flycatcher, Alder Flycatcher, and Swamp Sparrow.

Lookout Trail

This trail starts at km 39.7 on Highway 60. In addition to magnificent views of the Western Uplands, this 2.1-kilometre loop trail may offer soaring Broad-winged Hawks and Common Ravens. Hermit Thrush and Dark-eyed Junco nest along the cliff.

Ringneck Pond

Check carefully among the aquatic vegetation of this pond at km 41.2 on Highway 60 for Wood Duck, Ring-necked Duck, and Hooded Merganser, especially in late summer and fall. You should pull well off the highway on the shoulder here.

Spruce Bog Boardwalk

This is a 1.5-kilometre loop trail located at km 42.5 on Highway 60. Its extensive boardwalk sections allow the most accessible birding for "northern" species in the Highway 60 corridor. Search along the trail and its bordering open spruce and balsam fir forest for Spruce Grouse, Olive-sided Flycatcher, Yellow-bellied Flycatcher, Gray Jay, Boreal Chickadee, and Hermit Thrush. Sunday Creek and the adjoining bog here may have American Bittern, Ring-necked Duck, Northern Harrier, and Lincoln's Sparrow. The forest and bog habitat on the south side of Highway 60, opposite Spruce Bog Boardwalk, can be excellent for all these species as well, but there is no trail there and keeping your sense of direction in the dense cover can be a challenge.

Algonquin Visitor Centre

This magnificent facility is on a hilltop overlooking Sunday Creek bog and is accessible by a driveway at km 43 on Highway 60. The Visitor Centre feeders operate from late fall through winter into early spring and provide great views of winter finches and other birds. The centre is open only on weekends during that period but birders may be able to enter the building on weekdays to observe the feeders.

Beaver Pond Trail

Located at km 45.2 on Highway 60, it is 2 kilometres in length and passes through beaver meadow habitat favoured by birds such as American Bittern, Great Blue Heron, American Black Duck, Broad-winged Hawk, Eastern Kingbird, Common Yellowthroat, Swamp Sparrow and Red-winged Blackbird. Check shallow Amikeus Lake at Post 6 during fall for Green-winged Teal, Ring-necked Duck, Hooded Merganser, and occasional shorebirds.

Opeongo Road

Turn onto this road at km 46.3 on Highway 60. The paved road travels 6.2 kilometres north to Lake Opeongo Access Point through extensive areas of bog, sedge marsh, and black spruce forest. Birds likely to be found include American Bittern, Ring-necked Duck, Hooded Merganser, Northern Harrier, Spruce Grouse, Black-backed Woodpecker, Olive-sided Flycatcher, Alder Flycatcher, Gray Jay, Boreal Chickadee, Swainson's Thrush, Hermit Thrush, and Lincoln's Sparrow. Opeongo Road is usually plowed in winter as far as a locked gate where Gray Jays, Black-capped Chickadees, and winter finches gather for the seed left by birders.

Algonquin Logging Museum

This facility tells the interesting history of logging in Algonquin Park. Enter the parking lot from km 54.5 on Highway 60. Follow the 1.3-kilometre interpretive trail to look for Merlin, Hermit Thrush, and Gray Jay. Check the pond along the trail for Great Blue Heron, Wood Duck, Ring-necked Duck, and Hooded Merganser.

Barron Canyon Road:

This road is reached as follows: on the Highway 17 bypass, 3.5 kilometres west of the Forest Lea Road (approximately 9 kilometres west of Pembroke), turn south on County Road 26 (Doran Road). Travel 300 metres, then turn right onto County Road 28 (Barron Canyon Road) and drive 26 kilometres on pavement and then gravel to the Sand Lake Gate at the Algonquin Park boundary. The Barron Canyon Road passes through typical "east side" forests of Algonquin, featuring birch, poplar, and extensive stands of pine (red, white, and jack). It is open to the public all the way to Lake Travers on the Petawawa River, and the numbers and types of birds are often quite different from those seen on Highway 60. There are good birding opportunities all along this road, with species such as Yellow-bellied Sapsucker, Pileated Woodpecker, Gray Jay, Brown Creeper, Pine Warbler, and Red Crossbill being common. The following areas are particularly worthy of a stop, and may be located by referring to the kilometre signs along the road margin (e.g., Sand Lake Gate is at km 17.5).

Barron Canyon Trail

This 1.5-kilometre loop trail starts at km 28.9 on Barron Canyon Road. Hermit Thrush occurs along the trail, and listen for Yellow-bellied Flycatcher, Northern Waterthrush, and Common Yellowthroat singing in the spectacular canyon. Eastern Phoebes nest on the vertical rock bordering the river, far below.

Achray

Turn left at km 37.8 on Barron Canyon Road and proceed west for 4.8 kilometres to Achray Campground on Grand Lake. In spring and fall, check the lake by telescope for waterfowl and gulls, and look for shorebirds along the beaches. The campground can be good for Pine Warbler and Red Crossbill. Eastern Whip-poor-wills are often heard at night.

Hydro Line

The Barron Canyon Road intersects this major hydro transmission corridor at km 50. The open field habitat here may have Red-tailed Hawk, American Kestrel, Eastern Bluebird, and Field Sparrow.

Lake Travers

The extensive open jack pine forest from km 65 to 70 on the Barron Canyon Road may produce American Kestrel, Merlin, Spruce Grouse, Hermit Thrush, Lincoln's Sparrow, and Dark-eyed Junco. Common Nighthawks

and Eastern Whip-poor-wills
are regular here at dusk and
at night. From the Poplar
Rapids bridge just beyond km
72, check the Petawawa River
where it enters Lake Travers
for Common Merganser and
Red-breasted Merganser.
Lake Travers itself is often
good in spring and fall for
migrant waterbirds, including
Horned Grebe, Red-necked
Grebe, both scaup, Long-tailed
Duck, scoters, Bufflehead,
and Common Goldeneye.
Both Osprey and Bald Eagle
are frequently observed over
Lake Travers. The marsh near
the radio observatory may
have ducks and shorebirds
in September, and Nelson's
Sparrows in the first half of
October.

Water Birds

With a wide variety of different
habitats and many excellent birding sites, southern Ontario
offers birders a wealth of opportunities to see waterfowl and
shorebird species, both residents and migrants.

The southern Great Lakes shorelines are favourite feeding grounds for many gulls, shorebirds, waders and ducks.
Shores, mudflats, and marshy areas associated with lakes,
rivers, flooded fields, ponds, and even municipal sewage
lagoons are home to many water birds. In the spring and fall,
birders can enjoy one migration, one of the wonders of nature.
Migrants, among them ducks, geese and many shorebirds,
travel thousands of miles between their breeding grounds in
the north and their winter homes in the south. Along the way,
they stop to feed and to wait out inclement weather. These are
perfect times to go birding.

The birds in this section are those that you are most likely
to see in one of these habitats. Along with each full-colour
illustration, there are visual keys depicting seasonal range,
the size of the bird, the type of foot, its flight pattern and its
characteristic way of feeding. The egg is shown for birds that
breed in the province.

Common Loon
Gavia immer

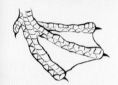

Size Identification

Foot: Tridactyl

Flying

Feeding

Egg: 75%

Observation Calendar

J F M A M J J A S O N D

Male/Female: *Summer*: Black head and neck with white banded neck ring; thick grey sharp bill; red eye; white chest and belly; black back and wings spotted white; feet and legs black. *Winter*: Contrasting blacks and whites muted to dark dull brown. *In flight*: Large feet trail behind tail feathers; quick wing beats close to water's surface; takes off from water by running across surface.

Did you know? Loons can remain underwater for more than 5 minutes. They dive to feed and to avoid danger.

Voice: Drawn out *lou-lou-lou-lou* like yodelling, often at dusk or dawn.
Food: Small fish.
Nest/Eggs: Mound built with aquatic plants, mostly on islands. 2 eggs.

Pied-billed Grebe

Podilymbus podiceps

Size Identification

Foot: Tridactyl

Flying

Feeding

Observation Calendar

J F M A M J J A S O N D

Male/Female: *Summer*: Overall brown with grey-brown back; yellow eye ring; stout bill, white with distinct black band; black chin; short tail. *Winter*: White ring on bill softens; lighter chin. White tail feathers occasionally revealed when threatened by another bird. *In flight*: White patch on belly and white trail edge on wings.

Voice: Call is *cow* repeated with *keeech* at end, also various cluckings.
Food: Small fish, amphibians, crayfish, aquatic insects.
Nest/Eggs: Platform built with aquatic plants in shallow water attached to reeds and other aquatic plants. 5-7 eggs.

Egg: Actual Size

Horned Grebe

Podiceps auritus

Size Identification

Foot: Tridactyl

Flying

Feeding

Observation Calendar
J F M A M J J A S O N D

Male/Female: *Summer*: Dark wings and head; distinct golden ear tufts; reddish-brown neck and sides; white belly; feet and legs black; red eye. *Winter*: Dark grey upperparts; large white patch on cheek extending to back of head.

Did you know? The Horned Grebe tends to jump forward from the water's surface before diving to catch prey.

Voice: Usually quiet but occasionally makes loud croaks and chatters.
Food: Small fish, aquatic insects, crayfish, shrimp, insects, frogs, salamanders.

Snow Goose

Chen caerulescens

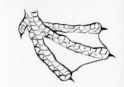

Foot: Tridactyl

Flying

Observation Calendar

J F M A M J J A S O N D

Male/Female: White overall with black primaries; short pink bill; feet and legs yellow; short tail.

Voice: High-pitched honk.
Food: Grains, seeds, grasses, aquatic plants, roots.

Feeding

31

Canada Goose
Branta canadensis

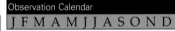

Observation Calendar

J F M A M J J A S O N D

Male/Female: Black head, neck and bill; white cheek patch; breast and belly pale brown with white flecks; feet and legs black; back and wings brown with white edging; short black tail; white rump, seen in flight. *In flight*: Flies in "V" formations.

Voice: Musical *honk*, repeated. Female slightly higher pitched *honk*.
Food: Grass, various seeds, sand, grain.
Nest/Eggs: Large nest of twigs, moss and grass, lined with down feathers, placed near water's edge. 4-8 eggs.

Mute Swan

Cygnus olor

Size Identification

Foot: Tridactyl

Flying

Feeding

Egg: 55%

Observation Calendar

J F M A M J J A S O N D

Male/Female: White overall; bright orange or pink beak; black knob at base of beak; unique S-shaped neck when swimming; feet and legs black.

Did you know? The Mute Swan, native to Europe, was brought to North America in the nineteenth century as an ornamental species for parks and large estates.

Voice: Mostly silent. Occasional hissing and barking or loud trumpet call.
Food: Fresh and saltwater plants, algae, grains.
Nest/Eggs: Large pile of grass and moss, lined with feathers, usually built on edge of pond or marsh. 4-6 eggs.

33

Trumpeter Swan

Cygnus buccinator

Observation Calendar
J F M A M J J A S O N D

Male/Female: Overall white; long neck; black bill; black skin extends from bill to eye; feet and legs black.

Voice: Bugle sounding *kah hah*.
Food: Aquatic plants, duckweed.
Nest/Eggs: Large platform built with twigs and other vegetation, near water. Often built on top of muskrat mounds or beaver dens. 4-6 eggs.

Tundra Swan

Cygnus columbianus

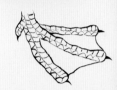

Size Identification

Foot: Tridactyl

Flying

Observation Calendar

J F M A M J J A S O N D

Male/Female: Overall white bird; black beak; yellow dash extending from eye down to base of beak, but not always present; black facial area narrowing to eyes; neck and head occasionally appear lightly rusted colour; feet and legs black.

Voice: High-pitched whistling. Bugling sound; *hoo-ho-hoo* when migrating.

Feeding

Food: Aquatic plants, mollusks, grains.

Nest/Eggs: Platform built of aquatic plants, grasses and moss, on islands. 2-7 eggs.

Wood Duck

Aix sponsa

Size Identification

Foot: Tridactyl

Flying

Observation Calendar

J F M A M J J A S O N D

Male: Green head and drooping crest; black cheeks; red eye and white throat with two spurs; bill orange with black markings; chest brown with white spots leading to white belly; black and green back; sides tan with white and black band. *In flight:* Long squared tail.

Female: Back and crown brown; white eye ring; speckled breast and lighter coloured belly.

Voice: Male — high-pitched whistle. Female — loud *oooooeeek* in flight.

Food: Aquatic plants, insects, minnows, amphibians.

Nest/Eggs: In cavity of tree, as high as 20 metres, or in a log or built structure lined with wood chips and feathers. 9-12 eggs.

Feeding

Egg: Actual Size

Gadwall

Anas strepera

Size Identification

Foot: Tridactyl

Flying

Feeding

Observation Calendar

J F M A M J J A S O N D

Male: Body overall grey-brown; black rump and tail feathers; light grey pointed feathers on back; feet and legs orange; thin black banding over entire body; black bill.

Female: Dull greyish brown and black overall; black bill with orange on sides.

Voice: Male gives whistle and *rab rab* call. Quacking and high-pitched descending note from female.

Food: Seeds and aquatic plants.

Nest/Eggs: Nest built on islands from plant material and lined with down, slightly concealed. 7-13 eggs.

Egg: Actual Size

37

American Wigeon

Anas americana

Observation Calendar

J F M A M J J A S O N D

Male: White patch running up forehead from bill; green around eye broadening at cheeks and descending on neck; brown changing to black on back and extremely pointed wings; pointed tail feathers are black, with white lines; bill white with black patches on top and on tip. *In flight*: Green on trailing edge of wing; white forewing and belly.
Female: Overall light brown with brighter colour running down sides. No green patch on eye.

Did you know? The American Wigeon is an opportunist: waiting for other diving ducks to come to the surface with their catch, it will attempt to steal the food.

Voice: Male — occasional distinctive whistle *wh-wh-whew*. Female quacks.
Food: Aquatic plants.
Nest/Eggs: Grasses lined with down, concealed under brush or tree, a distance from water. 9-12 eggs.

American Black Duck

Anas rubripes

Size Identification

Foot: Tridactyl

Flying

Feeding

Observation Calendar

J F M A M J J A S O N D

Male: Dark black with hint of brown overall and blue speculum; bill is olive; feet and legs orange. *In flight*: White patches under wings.
Female: Overall lighter brown than male with orange and black bill.

Voice: Both female and male *quack*. Male also whistles.
Food: Vegetation, insects, amphibians, snails, seed, grain, berries.
Nest/Eggs: Depression on ground, lined with grass, leaves and down, close to water's edge. 8-12 eggs.

Egg: Actual Size

Mallard

Anas platyrhynchos

Size Identification

Foot: Tridactyl

Flying

Feeding

Male: Bright green iridescent head, yellow bill; thin white collar; chestnut brown chest; grey sides; black and grey back; white tail; black curled feathers over rump; feet and legs orange. *In flight*: Blue speculum with white border, under-parts of wings grey and brown.
Female: Overall brown streaked with orange bill, black patches on bill; white tail feathers.

Voice: Male — call soft *raeb* repeated. Female — loud *quacks* repeated.
Food: Aquatic plants, grain, insects.
Nest/Eggs: Shallow cup built of grasses and aquatic plants, lined with feathers on ground concealed near water. 8-10 eggs.

Egg: Actual Size

Blue-winged Teal

Anas discors

Observation Calendar

J F M A M J J A S O N D

Male: Grey head with crescent-shaped white patch running up face, bill black; chest and belly brown; back and wings dark brown with buff highlights; blue and green speculum; feet and legs yellow.
Female: Overall brown speckled with pale blue speculum.

Voice: Male has high-pitched *peeeep*. Female — *quack* is soft and high-pitched.
Food: Aquatic plants, seeds.
Nest/Eggs: Pile of grasses lined with down, close to water's edge, concealed. 9-12 eggs.

Northern Shoveler

Anas clypeata

Size Identification

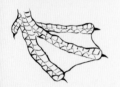

Foot: Tridactyl

Flying

Feeding

Observation Calendar

J F M A M J J A S O N D

Male: Grey speckled head and neck; yellow eye; wide black bill; sides rust; mottled brown back. *In flight:* Green speculum; light blue wing patch.
Female: Overall brown with orange bill.

Voice: Low *quack* or *cluck*.
Food: Aquatic plants, duckweed, insects.
Nest/Eggs: Made from grasses in hollow on ground, lined with down feathers, at a distance from water. 8-12 eggs.

Egg: Actual Size

Northern Pintail

Anas acuta

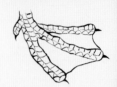

Foot: Tridactyl

Flying

Feeding

Observation Calendar

J F M A M J J A S O N D

Male: Brown head with white line circling around cheeks to chest; white chest and belly; back and wings are black and grey; long tail is black and brown; rump black; sides grey with thin black banding; bill grey with white line. *In flight*: Long tail; white neck and line running up neck.
Female: Overall brown with black bill; no pintail feature.

Voice: Male has two high-pitched whistles. Female quacks.
Food: Aquatic plants, seeds, crustaceans, corn, grains.
Nest/Eggs: Bowl of sticks, twigs, and grasses, lined with down, at a distance from water's edge. 6-9 eggs.

Egg: Actual Size

Green-winged Teal

Anas crecca

Size Identification

Foot: Tridactyl

Flying

Feeding

Observation Calendar
J F M A M J J A S O N D

Male: Head is rust with green patch running around eye to back of head; bill black; black at back of base of neck; warm grey body with thin black banding; distinctive white bar running down side just in front of wing; white rump; short square tail.
Female: Overall dull brown with green speculum; dark band running through eye.

Voice: Male — high pitched whistle. Female — weak shrill voice.
Food: Seeds, aquatic plants, corn, wheat, oats.
Nest/Eggs: On ground, cup shaped, filled with grasses and weeds, sometimes a distance from water. 10-12 eggs.

Egg: Actual Size

Canvasback

Aythya valisineria

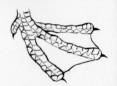

Observation Calendar

J F M A M J J A S O N D

Male: Dark reddish-brown head with sloping forehead; long black bill; black breast; grey wings; black tail; feet and legs black.
Female: Grey body; head and neck lighter brown.

Voice: Call is cooooing from male only. Female call is soft *krrr-krr* during courtship.
Food: Aquatic plants, roots, bulbs, insects, small fish, crustaceans.
Nest/Eggs: Bowl-like nest built from grasses and reeds then lined with feather down. Nest floats attached to aquatic plants. 7-12 eggs.

Redhead

Aythya americana

Observation Calendar

J F M A M J J A S O N D

Male: Deep red head; bluish bill with black tip; grey mottled overall; black breast.
Female: Brown body overall; dark brown back; white eye ring; darker crown.

Did you know? Females often lay their eggs in the nests of other ducks. Success is low because the host duck often deserts those eggs.

Voice: Male catlike during courtship.Female has soft growl.
Food: Aquatic vegetation, insects, larvae, molluscs, small crustaceans.
Nest/Eggs: Basket attached to aquatic plants such as cattails. 9-13 eggs.

Ring-necked Duck
Aythya collaris

Observation Calendar

J F M A M J J A S O N D

Male: Back, head and breast black; high forehead; black bill with white outlines; yellow eyes; white spur on breast leading to grey underside and belly. *In flight*: Grey speculum; white belly.

Female: Grey cheeks and bill; one white band at tip of bill; white eye ring; dark charcoal back; brown chest, belly and sides.

Voice: Male has low, loud whistle. Female call is soft *prrrrrrrrr* notes. Mostly quiet.

Food: Aquatic plants, molluscs, insects.

Nest/Eggs: Cup-shaped, built of grasses and moss and lined with down feathers, concealed near pond. 8-12 eggs.

Greater Scaup

Aythya marila

Size Identification

Foot: Tridactyl

Flying

Feeding

Observation Calendar

J F M A M J J A S O N D

Male: *Winter*: Dark green iridescent head, neck and chest; white sides and belly; large flat grey bill; yellow eye; grey back with thin black banding; stubby black tail; black feet and legs. *Summer*: Sides and belly brown; head, neck and chest dull brown-black. *In flight*: Large white patches on inside of wings.

Female: Overall dark brown with white face patch. Head held lower than male. *In flight*: Large white patches on trailing edge of wings.

Voice: Male — repeated *waaahooo*. Female — growling *arrrrr*. Mostly quiet.

Food: Aquatic plants, crustaceans, molluscs, snails.

Lesser Scaup

Aythya affinis

Size Identification

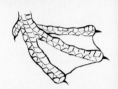

Foot: Tridactyl

Flying

Feeding

Observation Calendar

J F M A M J J A S O N D

Male: Black head comes to peak at top toward back; head has purple tint in bright lighting; yellow eye; short narrow grey bill; dark breast and neck; grey-banded back; white sides and belly; dark rump and tail; feet and legs black.

Female: Dark brown overall with white patches on either side of bill. *In flight*: Long white banding down to tip on underside of wings.

Did you know? Large flocks, called "rafts," gather together by the thousands on the water in the winter.

Voice: Single note, low whistle, *wheeeooo*, and quacking.

Food: Aquatic seeds, crustaceans, insects, snails.

49

Surf Scoter

Melanitta perspicillata

Size Identification

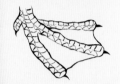

Foot: Tridactyl

Flying

Feeding

Observation Calendar

J F M A M J J A S O N D

Male: Overall black with white patches on forehead and back of neck; yellow eye; distinctive large orange and red bill with black and white patches on sides.

Female: Overall dark brown with large black bill and vertical white patch behind it; top of head is slightly darker. *In flight:* Pale grey belly.

Did you know? Spotting the Surf Scoter is easy if you look for birds diving directly into the breaking surf hunting for molluscs or crustaceans.

Voice: Male — low whistle during courtship.
Food: Mussels, crustaceans, insects, aquatic plants.

White-winged Scoter

Melanitta fusca

Observation Calendar

J F M A M J J A S O N D

Male: Black overall with yellow eye and white tear-shaped mark around eye; bill is orange, yellow and white; orange feet and legs. *In flight*: White wing patch.
Female: Brown overall; white oval on face; white patches on wings.

Voice: Male — in courtship is similar to ring of bell.
Female — low whistle.
Food: Clams, scallops, mussels.

Black Scoter

Melanitta nigra

Size Identification

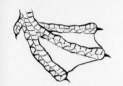

Foot: Tridactyl

Flying

Observation Calendar

J F M A M J J A S O N D

Feeding

Male: Overall black with long thin tail feathers; large yellow knob on top of black bill; feet and legs dark orange.
Female: Overall dark grey with lighter grey on cheeks.

Voice: Low whistle during courtship. Quiet.
Food: Aquatic plants, molluscs, mussels, limpets.

Long-tailed Duck

Clangula hyemalis

Observation Calendar

J F M A M J J A S O N D

Male: *Winter*: White head with grey cheek and black patch; bill black with tan band; white back with black and tan markings; black chest and white belly; very long tail feathers.
Female: *Winter*: White face, black crown; back brown with black wings; chest brown and white belly.

Voice: Male — call during courtship sounds similar to yodelling. Female — soft grunting and quacking.
Food: Insect larvae, molluscs, crustaceans.

Bufflehead

Bucephala albeola

Size Identification

Foot: Tridactyl

Flying

Feeding

Observation Calendar

J F M A M J J A S O N D

Male: Small compact duck; black head with large white patch behind the eye; grey bill; black back with white underparts.
Female: Grey-brown overall with smaller white patch behind the eye.

Voice: Mostly quiet. Male whistles. Female quacks.
Food: Small fish, crustaceans, snails and other molluscs.

Common Goldeneye

Bucephala clangula

Foot: Tridactyl

Flying

Feeding

Observation Calendar

| J F M A M J J A S O N D |

Male: Black/green head with round white patch on cheek, close to black bill; back black with white bars; underside white; orange feet and legs. *In flight*: Large white speculum.
Female: Brown head and light charcoal overall; bill black with yellow patch; white patches on back. Both male and female are stocky with large head.

Voice: Call during courtship *jeeeeent*. Wings whistle when in flight. Female — low grating sound in flight.
Food: Molluscs, crustaceans, aquatic insects.
Nest/Eggs: In tree cavity or built structure, lined with down. 8-12 eggs.

Hooded Merganser

Lophodytes cucullatus

Size Identification

Foot: Tridactyl

Flying

Feeding

Observation Calendar
J F M A M J J A S O N D

Male: Black crested head with large white patch on back of head behind eye; black bill is long and thin; rust eye; black back with rust sides and white underparts; black band runs down side into chest; white bands on black wings; tail is often cocked. *In flight*: Rapid energetic wing beats.
Female: Grey breast and belly; faint rust on back of crest; wings dark brown.

Voice: Call is low croaking or *gack*.
Food: Small fish, reptiles, crustaceans, molluscs, aquatic insects.
Nest/Eggs: In tree cavity or built structure, lined with grasses and down feathers, occasionally on ground. 9-12 eggs.

Egg: Actual Size

Common Merganser

Mergus merganser

Foot: Tridactyl

Flying

Feeding

Observation Calendar

J F M A M J J A S O N D

Male: Dark green head crested, with red toothed bill slightly hooked at end; white ring around neck connects to white chest and belly; black back and white sides; feet and legs orange.
Female: Brown head and grey-brown back; white chin.

Voice: Male call is *twaang*. Female call is series of hard notes.
Food: Small fish, crustaceans, molluscs.
Nest/Eggs: Built of reeds and grass and lined with down feathers in tree cavity, rock crevice, on ground or in built structure. 8-11 eggs.

Egg: Actual Size

Red-breasted Merganser

Mergus serrator

Observation Calendar

J F M A M J J A S O N D

Male: *Winter*: Dark green and black head with crest; red eye; white neck ring; long orange toothed bill with slight hook at end; chest white, spotted black; back black with white patching. *Summer*: Head chestnut brown; overall body grey. *In flight*: Rapid wing beats; straight flying pattern; dark breast on male.

Female: Brown head with grey upper parts and white belly.

Voice: Call for male is *eoooow* usually during courtship. Female — series of hard notes. Mostly quiet.

Food: Small fish, molluscs, crustaceans.

Nest/Eggs: Built of grass and down, in sheltered area under bush. 8-10 eggs.

Ruddy Duck

Oxyura jamaicensis

Size Identification

Foot: Tridactyl

Flying

Feeding

Observation Calendar

J F M A M J J A S O N D

Male: Distinct broad light blue bill; black cap running down back of neck; white cheeks; reddish-brown body; long black tail that is often held upright.
Female: Overall brown with white cheeks; buff line just below eyes; beak is black.

Voice: Mostly quiet except for drumming and clicking sounds by male during courting.
Food: Aquatic plants, crustaceans, aquatic insects.
Nest/Eggs: Floating nest of dry plant material, lined with down and hidden amongst reeds. 6-20 eggs.

Egg: Actual Size

Double-crested Cormorant

Phalacrocorax auritus

Size Identification

Foot: Tridactyl

Flying

Feeding

Observation Calendar
J F M A M J J A S O N D

Male/Female: Overall black with long tail feathers; bright orange chin and throat patch; feet and legs black. Crest is visible only during courtship. *In flight*: Neck is kinked. Often seen flying extremely high.

Did you know? Cormorants are often seen perched on a rock or pier with wings fully extended to dry their feathers.

Voice: Call is a variety of grunts and croaks, only at its nest. Elsewhere silent.
Food: Small fish.
Nest/Eggs: Colonies. Platform built of sticks and twigs, lined with leaves and grass and placed on ground or small tree. 3-5 eggs.

Egg: Actual Size

60

American Bittern

Botaurus lentiginosus

Foot: Anisodactyl

Flying

Feeding

Observation Calendar
J F M A M J J A S O N D

Male/Female: Overall reddish brown with white stripes on underside; yellow bill long and sharp; short brown tail lightly banded; smudgy brown back. *In flight*: Tips of wings dark brown.

Did you know? The American Bittern is extremely difficult to spot in the field because, if approached, it will freeze and blend into the reeds.

Voice: In flight, a loud *squark*. Song is a loud *kong-chu-chunk*, on breeding grounds.
Food: Small fish, reptiles, amphibians, insects, small mammals.
Nest/Eggs: Concealed platform built from aquatic plants just above water. 2-6 eggs.

Egg: Actual Size

Least Bittern
Ixobrychus exilis

Foot: Anisodactyl

Flying

Feeding

Observation Calendar
J F M A M J J A S O N D

Male: Black crown and back; long sharp yellow bill; white chin, chest and belly with reddish tints on sides; dark yellow feet and legs.
Female: Dark crown.

Did you know? You will seldom see a Least Bittern — it is very shy and secretive. If approached it will freeze in position.

Food: Small fish, reptiles.
Voice: Call is sharp *keeek* repeated. Song is soft *kuuu*.
Nest/Eggs: Platform nest built of sticks with grass on top, hidden amongst water plants. 2-7 eggs.

Egg: Actual Size

Great Blue Heron

Ardea herodias

Size Identification

Foot: Anisodactyl

Flying

Feeding

Observation Calendar

J F M A M J J A S O N D

Male/Female: Overall grey-blue with black crest on top of head; long neck and bill; black patch connecting eye and long yellow bill; white head; long grey legs and feet; long feathers extend over wings and base of neck. *In flight*: Neck is kinked; legs extend past tail; constant wing flapping with occasional glide.

Voice: Bill makes clacking sound. Call is harsh *squawk*.
Food: Small fish, reptiles, amphibians, crustaceans, birds, aquatic insects.
Nest/Eggs: Colonies. Platform of aquatic plants and twigs, lined with softer materials such as down and soft grass, placed in tree or shrub. 3-7 eggs.

Egg: Actual Size

Size Identification

Foot: Anisodactyl

Flying

Feeding

Egg: 90%

Great Egret
Ardea alba

Observation Calendar
J F M A M J J A S O N D

Male/Female: Overall large white bird; long sharp yellow bill; long black legs and feet; long thin neck; small head; thin feathers off tail; bright yellow eyes.

Did you know? During courtship Great Egrets will clack their bills together while making various head movements and dancing.

Voice: Series of low-pitched *coos*.
Food: Fish, amphibians, insects, small mammals.
Nest/Eggs: Platform nest poorly built of twigs and sticks, in trees or large bushes. Occasionally built in cattails. 1-6 eggs.

Green Heron

Butorides virescens

Size Identification

Foot: Anisodactyl

Flying

Feeding

Observation Calendar

J F M A M J J A S O N D

Male/Female: Distinct reddish-brown cheeks, neck, chest and belly; black cap; black wings with thin white streaking; broad sharp black bill with slight amounts of yellow; yellow eye; feet and legs yellow or orange; white patch above eye and running along base of bill.

Did you know? The Green Heron has been observed placing a twig on the water as bait for prey. When prey approaches the twig the heron strikes quickly with its sharp bill.

Voice: Typical call is sharp *kiew*. When aggressive will call *raah*.
Food: Fish, insects, small amphibians, crabs.
Nest/Eggs: Flat nest built of twigs and sticks, placed in tree or bush. 3-6 eggs.

Egg: Actual Size

Black-crowned Night Heron

Nycticorax nycticorax

Observation Calendar

J F M A M J J A S O N D

Male/Female: Adult has dark grey upperparts; middle grey wings; light grey chin, chest and belly; black cap; broad sharp black bill; short yellow legs and feet; red eye. Immature is heavily streaked with brown.

Did you know? During breeding dances the two birds extend their necks horizontally and raise their head feathers, while gently touching bills together.

Food: Fish, amphibians, insects, small mammals, occasionally young birds.
Voice: Very rough-sounding low *quok*, usually at dusk. *Roc roc* sound while nesting.
Nest/Eggs: Flat nest built of twigs and aquatic plants then lined with finer plant materials, placed high in shrub or tree. Occasionally on the ground. 3-5 eggs.

Virginia Rail

Rallus limicola

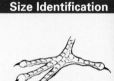

Size Identification

Foot: Anisodactyl

Flying

Feeding

Observation Calendar

J F M A M J J A S O N D

Male/Female: Chicken-like; grey head banded dark charcoal on top; eye red; neck and sides rich rust; long curved red and black bill; back dark brown with rust edging; wings rust with black; short black and brown tail; legs and feet red; belly black and white banding.

Voice: Call is descending *kicket* repeated with grunting notes.
Food: Marine worms, snails, aquatic insects.
Nest/Eggs: Cup of grass and reeds built slightly above water's surface, attached to reeds and other aquatic plant life. 5-12 eggs.

Egg: Actual Size

Sora
Porzana carolina

Size Identification

Foot: Anisodactyl

Flying

Feeding

Egg: Actual Size

Observation Calendar
J F M A M J J A S O N D

Male/Female: Chicken-like; grey above eye runs down to chin, breast and belly; black mask behind thick yellow bill; upper parts chestnut brown with white and dark brown bars; legs and feet yellow; buff rump.

Did you know? The Sora, like other rails, prefers to migrate at night.

Voice: Call is musical *kuur weeee,* which is repeated and descends.
Food: Aquatic insects, seeds.
Nest/Eggs: Built in open marsh, attached to reeds, using leaves and grass. 6-15 eggs.

Common Moorhen

Gallinula chloropus

Size Identification

Foot: Anisodactyl

Flying

Feeding

Egg: Actual Size

Observation Calendar
J F M A M J J A S O N D

Male/Female: *Summer*: Overall dark body; bright red forehead and bill; yellow bill tip; white tail feathers at rump; white line of feathers along wing edge; large yellow feet and legs. *Winter*: Red forehead and bill become brownish-yellow.

Did you know? If broods are born close together the first brood will often help with the feeding of the second.

Voice: Similar to chicken clucks, but also makes a variety of sounds including short gravelly noises.
Food: Grasses, seeds, snails, aquatic insects, land insects.
Nest/Eggs: Platform nest built from grasses, over water and attached to aquatic plants. 4-17 eggs.

American Coot
Fulica americana

Size Identification

Foot: Anisodactyl

Flying

Feeding

Egg: Actual Size

Observation Calendar
J F M A M J J A S O N D

Male/Female: Duck-like body, slate-coloured overall; white bill and frontal shield shows red swelling at close range; partial black ring around tip of beak; feet and legs greenish-yellow; lobed toes.

Did you know? The American Coot has many different courtship displays, including running over the surface of water with its neck and head bent very low.

Voice: Variety of calls including clucks, grunts and other harsh notes and toots sounding like a small trumpet.
Food: Seeds, leaves, roots, small aquatic plants.
Nest/Eggs: Floating platform nest of dead leaves and stems, lined with finer material and anchored to reeds. 8-10 eggs.

Sandhill Crane

Grus canadensis

Size Identification

Foot: Anisodactyl

Flying

Feeding

Observation Calendar

J F M A M J J A S O N D

Male/Female: Overall white; dark red patch on forehead; long neck; long sharp black bill; some feathers on back may have rust colouring; tail feathers droop down at end; long legs and feet yellow.

Voice: Loud resonant rolling bugle.
Food: Seeds, grains, small mammals, reptiles, frogs, insects.
Nest/Eggs: Large platform nest built of grasses, twigs, aquatic plants and weeds, on ground or possibly in shallow water. 1-3 eggs.

Egg: 80%

Black-bellied Plover
Pluvialis squatarola

Size Identification

Foot: Anisodactyl

Flying

Feeding

Observation Calendar
J F M A M J J A S O N D

Male/Female: : Black mask set against pale grey speckled head, crown and neck; bill black; breast and belly black; wings and tail black with white speckles; white rump; feet and legs black. : Black face patch; dull grey-brown chest and belly. : Black on inner wings underparts; white wing band; white rump.

Voice: Call is whistled three-note.
Food: Worms, insects, crustaceans, molluscs, seeds.

Semipalmated Plover
Charadrius semipalmatus

Size Identification

Foot: Anisodactyl

Flying

Feeding

Observation Calendar

J F M A M J J A S O N D

Male/Female: *Summer*: Dark brown head, back and wings; small white patch on forehead with black band above; faint white eyebrow; white chin extending into white collar with black collar band below; chest and belly white; wing feathers black; feet and legs orange; bill is orange, tipped in black. *In flight*: Quick wingbeats with slight glide just before landing.

Voice: Whistle *chee-weee* with a defensive call in quick short notes. Also soft rattling.
Food: Marine worms.
Nest/Eggs: Hollow on ground with shell bits and grass, on sand or gravel. 4 eggs.

Killdeer

Charadrius vociferus

Size Identification

Foot: Anisodactyl

Flying

Feeding

Observation Calendar
J F M A M J J A S O N D

Male/Female: Bright red eye with black band running across forehead; white chin, collar and eyebrow; black collar ring under white; black chest band set against white chest and belly; back and wing rust and grey; wing tipped in black; legs and feet pink/grey. *In flight:* Orange rump; black wing tips and white band on trailing edge.

Did you know? A killdeer will exhibit a "broken-wing" display when a predator comes close to the nest sight. The bird will appear hurt and run around distracting the predator from the nest.

Voice: Variety of calls with most common being *kill deeee* which is repeated.
Food: Insects.
Nest/Eggs: Hollow on ground with some pebbles. Most popular sightings in gravel parking lots. 3-4 eggs.

Egg: Actual Size

Greater Yellowlegs

Tringa melanoleuca

Observation Calendar

J F M A M J J A S O N D

Male/Female: Speckled grey and white overall; long bright yellow legs and feet; long straight black bill; short tail feathers with black banding; white belly.

Voice: Call is whistled musical *whew* repeated and descending.

Food: Fish, snails, insects, plants.

Nest/Eggs: Hollow on ground in damp area. 4 eggs.

Lesser Yellowlegs

Tringa flavipes

Size Identification

Foot: Anisodactyl

Flying

Feeding

Observation Calendar

J F M A M J J A S O N D

Male/Female: Long black bill; dark upperparts speckled white; white belly; wings and tail feathers banded black; long yellow legs and feet.

Voice: Call is *tu* repeated.
Food: Insects, worms, snails, berries, small fish.

Solitary Sandpiper

Tringa solitaria

Size Identification

Foot: Anisodactyl

Flying

Feeding

Observation Calendar

J F M A M J J A S O N D

Male/Female: *Summer*: Overall dark brown with white spotting; streaked head and neck; white eye ring; long thin black bill; feet and legs dark grey; white belly and rump. *Winter*: Grey overall.

Voice: A series of three high-pitched notes *wheet wheet wheet*.
Food: Aquatic insects, crustaceans, insects, worms.

Spotted Sandpiper
Actitis macularia

Size Identification

Foot: Anisodactyl

Flying

Feeding

Observation Calendar

J F M A M J J A S O N D

Male/Female: *Summer*: Grey-brown on head, back and wings; white eyebrow and black line running from beak to back of neck; long orange bill; white chin, chest and belly with distinct charcoal spots; yellow feet and legs; bobbing tail.
Winter: White underparts — no spots. *In flight*: Quick stiff wingbeats, slightly arched back.

Voice: Quiet bird but makes a *peeetaawet* call during courtship and a whistle that is repeated when alarmed.
Food: Insects, worms, crustaceans, fish, flies, beetles.
Nest/Eggs: Shallow depression on ground, lined with grasses and mosses. 4 eggs.

Egg: Actual Size

Upland Sandpiper

Bartramia longicauda

Size Identification

Foot: Anisodactyl

Flying

Feeding

Observation Calendar

J F M A M J J A S O N D

Male/Female: Brown mottled overall; white belly; small head with long yellow and black bill; long neck and tail feathers; feet and legs yellow.

Did you know? Courtship dances include aerial and ground displays with occasional motions in which the bird holds its wing above its head.

Voice: Call is *pulip pulip* while in flight. Song is lilting double whistle, ascends then descends.
Food: Insects, worms.
Nest/Eggs: Depression in ground lined with fine grasses, in grassy areas such as fields or meadows. 4 eggs.

Egg: Actual Size

Size Identification

Foot: Anisodactyl

Flying

Feeding

Whimbrel

Numenius phaeopus

Observation Calendar

J F M A M J J A S O N D

Male/Female: Overall grey and brown speckled with cream; sides banded with dark brown; long downward curving black bill with yellow underside; cream eyebrow extending from bill; dark brown cap; feet and legs grey; tail brown with dark brown banding.

Voice: Inflight call is rapid *qui* repeated numerous times with no change in pitch.
Food: Insects, marine worms, crustaceans, mollusks, crabs, berries.

Ruddy Turnstone

Arenaria interpres

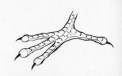

Observation Calendar

J F M A M J J A S O N D

Male/Female: *Winter*: Speckled brown back, head and wings; white belly, brown bib and white patch on either side; feet and legs dark orange. *Summer*: Overall upperparts brown and black; brown and black bill with white patch just behind bill; black bib with white patch; short black tail. *In flight*: White bands on wings and back.

Did you know? The Ruddy Turnstone got its name because of its feeding habits. The bird wanders down the feeding area turning over stones.

Voice: Call is *tuc e tuc*.
Food: Insects, molluscs, crustaceans, marine worms.

Red Knot

Calidris canutus

Size Identification

Foot: Anisodactyl

Flying

Feeding

Observation Calendar

J F M A M J J A S O N D

Male/Female: *Winter*: Face, neck and chest turn from brick red in summer to light grey; wings and tail turn dark; black bill; legs and feet charcoal.

Did you know? Red Knots are mostly seen flying in flocks of hundreds of birds with Dunlins, plovers, Godwits, sandpipers and many other shorebirds in their migration south or north.

Voice: Call is low *nuuuut*. Soft *currret* in flight.
Food: Molluscs, worms, insects, crabs, seeds.

Sanderling
Calidris alba

Size Identification

Foot: Anisodactyl

Flying

Feeding

Observation Calendar

J F M A M J J A S O N D

Male/Female: *Summer*: Bright brown and speckled on head, back and breast; black tail; white belly; long bill is dark brown; feet and legs black. *Winter*: Light grey head, neck and chest; white cheeks, white belly; tail black. *In flight*: White on underwing; white bar on top side of wing.

Voice: Call is *kip* in flight. Chattering during feeding.
Food: Crustaceans, molluscs, marine worms, insects.

Semipalmated Sandpiper

Calidris pusillus

Size Identification

Foot: Anisodactyl

Flying

Feeding

Observation Calendar

J F M A M J J A S O N D

Male/Female: Short, straight black bill; back is grey-brown; white underparts; black legs with slightly webbed front toes. In winter, uniformly grey on back. *In flight*: Distinctive formations of thousands of birds stretching hundreds of metres, showing white underparts in unison.

Voice: Continuous quavering *churrrk*.
Food: Small marine invertebrates, usually on mud flats.

Least Sandpiper

Calidris minutilla

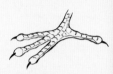

Size Identification

Foot: Anisodactyl

Flying

Feeding

Observation Calendar

J F M A M J J A S O N D

Male/Female: Long downward curved black bill; overall brown and black; belly and rump white; feet and legs are yellow. Overall colour turns grey in non-breeding seasons. *In flight*: V-shaped wings white on undersides.

Voice: High pitched *kreeeep* rising up. When in flock it gives high repeated notes.

Food: Insects, mollusks, crustaceans, marine worms.

Pectoral Sandpiper
Calidris melanotos

Size Identification

Foot: Anisodactyl

Flying

Feeding

Observation Calendar

J F M A M J J A S O N D

Male/Female: Overall dark brown with lighter buff trimming feathers; long thin bill dark grey with slight amount of orange, dipping slightly at tip; chest with dense brown streaking on white; belly and rump white; feet and legs greyish-yellow.

Did you know? During the mating season males pump up an air sack in the neck for a flight display to attract females.

Voice: In flight call is low hard *churrk*. Male mating call in flight similar to *ooo-ah*, repeated two or three times.
Food: Insects, worms, crabs, grass seeds.

Dunlin

Calidris alpina

Observation Calendar

J F M A M J J A S O N D

Male/Female: Long black bill; grey face with rust and black speckled crown; breast white speckled brown; dull brown wings and back; short black tail; feet and legs black. *In flight*: White underparts and wing feathers.

Did you know? Dunlins usually flock together performing wonderful aerial shows when flushed.

Voice: In flight call: soft *creeeep* or *chit-lit*.
Food: Crustaceans, molluscs, marine worms, insects.

Short-billed Dowitcher

Limnodromus griseus

Size Identification

Foot: Anisodactyl

Flying

Feeding

Observation Calendar

J F M A M J J A S O N D

Male/Female: : Rust neck and chest speckled black; back and wings dark brown speckled with buff; dark brown cap on head. : Grey speckled overall with dark, barred flanks; black bill fading to yellow near base, white eyebrows; black and brown tail feathers; feet and legs yellow.

Voice: Call is repeated several times in soft high-pitch.
Food: Marine worms, molluscs, insects.

Wilson's Snipe

Gallinago delicata

Foot: Anisodactyl

Flying

Feeding

Observation Calendar

J F M A M J J A S O N D

Male/Female: Very long narrow bill; small head and large brown/black eye; buff eye ring; black and white bars on white belly; brown back striped with pale yellow; short yellow feet and legs; tail has rust band. *In flight*: Pointed wings; flies in back and forth motion with quick wingbeats.

Did you know? The Wilson's Snipe uses its long bill to hunt in bog-like conditions where it can penetrate through the soft ground to catch prey below the surface.

Voice: Call is a *swheet swheet* with sharp *scaip* call when flushed.
Food: Larvae, crayfish, molluscs, insects, frogs, seeds.
Nest/Eggs: Hollow in marsh area, concealed with grass, leaves, twigs and moss. 4 eggs.

Egg: Actual Size

American Woodcock
Scolopax minor

Size Identification

Foot: Anisodactyl

Flying

Feeding

Observation Calendar
J F M A M J J A S O N D

Male/Female: Distinctive long, straight, narrow bill of light brown; large brown eyes set back on the head; overall brown-black back with buff underside; feet and legs pale pink. *In flight*: Short wings explode with clatter.

Did you know? When courtship is taking place, the males will rise up in the air and circle around as high as 15 metres.

Voice: A deep *peeeeint* and a tin whistle sounding twitter when in flight.
Food: Earthworms, a variety of insects and insect larvae, seeds.
Nest/Eggs: Shallow depression on ground, lined with dead leaves and needles, in wooded area. 4 eggs.

Egg: Actual Size

Wilson's Phalarope

Phalaropus tricolor

Observation Calendar

J F M A M J J A S O N D

Male: *Summer*: White throat; light rust on back of head changing to pale grey on breast; pale grey underparts; grey back and wings.

Female: *Summer*: Long thin black bill, white chin and cheeks turning rust running down white neck; black band runs from beak through eye down side of neck to back; grey cap; white sides and belly; grey feet and legs. *In flight*: White rump; no wing bands; long legs.

Male/Female: *Winter*: Similar to summer male with pale grey, not rust, on head and neck.

Did you know? This is one species where the male does all the nest tending. He builds the nest, incubates eggs and raises young.

Voice: Soft call is *aangh*.
Food: Insects, crustaceans.

Red-necked Phalarope

Phalaropus lobatus

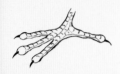

Foot: Anisodactyl

Flying

Feeding

Observation Calendar
J F M A M J J A S O N D

Male/Female: *Winter:* White and grey chest and belly. Face white with black mark behind eye; dark grey wings and back.
Male: *Summer:* Top of head black; long black bill; white chin; black band running under eye against white and rust; rust neck; grey chest changing to white belly; dark brown and rust wings and back; tail black; white rump.
Female: Overall similar markings except bolder colour; rufous neck with more contrast overall.

Voice: Call is sharp *twic*.
Food: Aquatic insects, molluscs, crustaceans.

Bonaparte's Gull

Larus philadelphia

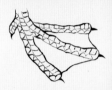

Observation Calendar

J F M A M J J A S O N D

Male/Female: *Summer:* Smaller gull with dark head and bill; white neck, chest and belly; grey back and black tail feathers. *Winter:* During winter months black cap disappears and a small black spot on side of head turns white. *In flight:* Wings appear black tipped.

Voice: Low rasping *gerrrr* or *wreeeek*.
Food: Small fish, worms, ground insects.

Ring-billed Gull

Larus delawarensis

Foot: Tridactyl

Flying

Feeding

Egg: Actual Size

Observation Calendar

J F M A M J J A S O N D

Male/Female: *Summer*: White overall; yellow bill with black band at end; yellow eye; pale grey wings and black tips and white patches within black tips; black feet and legs. *Winter*: Feet and legs turn yellow; light brown spots on top of head and back of neck. *In flight*: Grey underparts; black wing tips.

Voice: Loud *kaawk* and other calls.
Food: Insects, bird eggs, worms, garbage.
Nest/Eggs: Colonies. Grasses, sticks, twigs and pebbles, built on ground. 3 eggs.

94

Herring Gull

Larus argentatus

Size Identification

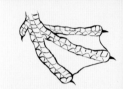

Foot: Tridactyl

Flying

Feeding

Observation Calendar

J F M A M J J A S O N D

Male/Female: White head that in winter is streaked light brown; yellow eye and bill; small red patch on lower bill; tail black; feet and legs red. *In flight*: Grey wing with white on trailing edge and black tips; pale brown rump; wide charcoal tail feathers.

Voice: Variety of squawks and squeals. Aggressive alarm call is *kak kak kak kak* ending in *yucca*.
Food: Insects, small mammals, clams, fish, small birds, crustaceans, mussels, rodents, garbage.
Nest/Eggs: Colonies. Mound lined with grass and seaweed on ground or cliff. Usually on islands. 2-4 eggs.

Egg: 90%

Iceland Gull

Larus glaucoides kumlieni

Size Identification

Foot: Tridactyl

Flying

Feeding

Observation Calendar
J F M A M J J A S O N D

Male/Female: Overall white with light grey back and wings; white wings underside; yellow bill with red tip on lower part; yellow eye; dark pink feet and legs. *In flight*: Overall white and grey underparts; white patches on wing tips.

Voice: Mostly quiet. Variety of squeaks.
Food: Fish, carrion, bird eggs.

Glaucous Gull
Larus hyperboreus

Size Identification

Foot: Tridactyl

Flying

Feeding

Observation Calendar

J F M A M J J A S O N D

Male/Female: Overall white with light grey back and wings; bill is yellow with red patch on lower portion at tip; yellow eye; pink legs and feet; short square white tail. *In flight*: White wing tips on grey wings.

Voice: Variety of squawks and other calls that are deep and hoarse sounding.
Food: Small mammals, birds, eggs, insects, garbage, small fish, crustaceans, carrion, molluscs.

Great Black-backed Gull
Larus marinus

Size Identification

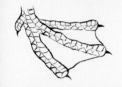

Foot: Tridactyl

Flying

Feeding

Observation Calendar
J F M A M J J A S O N D

Male/Female: White head, chin, chest and belly; red patch on lower portion of bill; feet and legs pink/grey; black wings with thin white band on trailing edge; tail and back black.
In flight: Pale grey undersides with black wing tips; tail white.

Voice: Loud squawks and deep guttural notes.
Food: Scavenger. Small fish, mammals, young birds and garbage. Major predator of other birds including puffin and tern chicks.
Nest/Eggs: Colonies. Mound of seaweed and other coastal plants, lined with grasses, on ground or rocky ledge. 3 eggs.

Egg: 80%

Caspian Tern

Sterna caspia

Observation Calendar

J F M A M J J A S O N D

Male/Female: Largest tern, with distinctive black cap; long sharp orange bill; white neck, chest and belly; grey back with long grey wings; short white tail; feet black. Juvenile feet often yellow.

Voice: Deep heronlike *aayayam* and harsh *cahar*.
Food: Small fish.
Nest/Eggs: Mostly nests in colonies. Nest is a depression in ground, lined with grass and seaweed, on a sandy beach. 2-3 eggs.

Common Tern
Sterna hirundo

Size Identification

Foot: Tridactyl

Flying

Feeding

Observation Calendar

J F M A M J J A S O N D

Male/Female: *Summer*: Soft grey overall with black cap; white cheeks; long thin red bill with black tip; short red feet and legs; wings and tail feathers grey, exceptionally long; white underside to tail. *Winter*: Black cap recedes leaving white face; black bar on wing; charcoal on tail. *In flight*: Charcoal on wing tips; grey overall; quick wingbeats.

Voice: Short *kip* repeated and louder *keeeear*.
Food: Small fish.
Nest/Eggs: Colonies. On ground, cup of grasses on sandy or pebbled areas. Most often on islands. 2-3 eggs.

Egg: Actual Size

Forster's Tern
Sterna forsteri

Foot: Tridactyl

Flying

Feeding

Observation Calendar
| J F M A M J J A S O N D |

Male: Overall white body with grey wings; distinct black cap; bright orange-red bill with black tip; grey and white tail extends slightly beyond folded wings; feet and legs orange.

Voice: Short calls including *keeer*, *zreeep* and *kip*.
Food: Fish, flying insects.
Nest/Eggs: Cavity scraped into ground on sandy or gravel beaches, often on islands. 3-4 eggs.

Egg: Actual Size

Black Tern

Childonias niger

Size Identification

Size Identification

Foot: Tridactyl

Flying

Feeding

Observation Calendar
J F M A M J J A S O N D

Male/Female: *Summer*: Black head, bill, chest and belly; white rump; feet and legs black; wings and tail charcoal. *Winter*: Wings and back charcoal; head white with black on top; white chest and underparts.

Did you know? This is one very fast bird. The Black Tern catches insects in flight.

Voice: Call is short *kirc* of *keeeel*.
Food: Insects.
Nest: Colonies. Loosely built pile of aquatic plants and grasses, on water's edge or floating on water. 3 eggs.

Egg: Actual Size

102

Land Birds

Many of the land birds described in the following pages can be seen anywhere in the southern part of Ontario. In woodlands and meadows, where songbirds and other small species such as chickadees, finches, flycatchers, nuthatches, sparrows and warblers abound, you are also likely to see hawks and other raptors.

In wilderness areas where habitat is less disturbed by human activity — especially in national and provincial parks — there are opportunities to see and hear some less common species. Park interpreters can provide specific information on the birds and hot spot areas to be found in each park.

Many species have adapted well to urban settings. In parks and suburban neighbourhoods, you can see a wide variety of year-round inhabitants. Birds can be attracted to your backyard by the type of tree, bushes and plants that are growing there. This book indicates those that will come to your backyard bird feeder and those that will make use of a nesting box. Each bird requires a different type of nesting box and you can learn more about making these by visiting birding web sites.

The visual keys in this section depict seasonal range — when you will see the bird — its size, the type of foot and the nesting location. The egg is shown for birds that breed in the province. The description emphasizes the distinctive markings of each bird, the food preferences and the calls or songs of each bird.

Size Identification

Foot: Anisodactyl

Egg: 60%

Turkey Vulture
Cathartes aura

Observation Calendar
J F M A M J J A S O N D

Male/Female: Large overall black bird; silver-grey underside of wings is seen in flight; naked red head; pale yellow sharply curved beak; feet and legs charcoal.

Did you know? Turkey vultures are most commonly seen soaring high over the countryside with their long wings held upward in a wide V-shape.

Voice: Grunts and hisses during aggression or feeding.
Food: Carrion.
Nest/Eggs: Nest made of scrap on ground, usually in cave, on cliff, hollow of tree or in fallen log. 1-3 eggs.

Nesting Location

Osprey
Pandion haliaetus

Size Identification

Foot: Anisodactyl

Egg: 70%

Observation Calendar

J F M A M J J A S O N D

Male/Female: In flight: White belly and chest; wings grey with black banding; white wing underparts connect to chest; black band running through eye; large black bill; tail grey with black banding. **Perched**: Black back and wings with thin white line running above wing; eye yellow with black band running through and down to cheek; chin white; top of head white with black patches.
Female: More streaked then male.

Voice: A loud chirp which trails off or ascending **squeeeee** during courtship displays.
Food: Various small fish.
Nest/Eggs: Constructed of twigs and sticks, lined with sod, grass and vines, in upper parts of trees and on top of poles, 60 feet above ground. 2-3 eggs.

Nesting Location

Size Identification

Foot: Anisodactyl

Egg: 70%

Nesting Location

Bald Eagle
Haliaeetus leucocephalus

Observation Calendar
J F M A M J J A S O N D

Male/Female: In flight: Broad black wings and belly with white head and tail feathers. **Perched**: White head with brilliant yellow eyes; white tail feathers; black back and wings; feet and legs yellow; bill yellow.
Juvenile: Mistaken for Golden Eagle because it lacks white head and tail; chest white and speckled; black wings with white speckles; underparts black with large areas of white.

Did you know? The eagle population is now recovering from rapid declines in the 1970s due to the widespread use of DDT.

Voice: A loud scream given in multiples.
Food: A variety of small and medium-sized mammals, fish and carrion.
Nest/Eggs: Upper parts of large, often dead, trees built with large twigs, lined with grass, moss, sod and weeds. 2 eggs.

Northern Harrier (Marsh Hawk)

Size Identification

Foot: Anisodactyl

Egg: 90%

Observation Calendar

J F M A M J J A S O N D

Male: In flight: White underside with black and rust speckles; head is grey; black on tips of wings; orange feet; wings are V-shaped in flight. **Perched**: Grey head with white face mask; yellow eyes; thin rust banding down front; white rump.
Female: Slightly larger than male with brown overall; buff face disk around cheeks; buff under chin and belly is banded with brown; bill grey; yellow eyes.

Did you know? While gliding over meadows, the Northern Harrier's wings take a V-shape, making it easy to identify.

Voice: Relatively quiet bird with occasional screams of alarm.
Food: A variety of small mammals and birds.
Nest/Eggs: On or near ground, built of sticks, straw and grasses. 4-5 eggs.

Nesting Location

Sharp-shinned Hawk

Accipiter striatus

Size Identification

Foot: Anisodactyl

Egg: Actual Size

Observation Calendar

J F M A M J J A S O N D

Male/Female: In flight: Small hawk with rust chest banded with buff; long square tail is white with charcoal banding; wings dark brown and rounded; top of head dark brown. **Perched**: Brick-red eyes with brown band just below eye; bill is black with yellow base; feet and legs yellow; white feathers extend out of rust-coloured belly.

Did you know? Over the past few years there has been a dramatic decrease in the eastern population. This may be directly related to the decrease in songbirds that it hunts.

Voice: A quick high pitched **kik kik kik**.
Food: Small songbirds.
Nest/Eggs: Broad platforms of twigs and sticks in conifers or deciduous trees built against the trunk, lined with bark. 4-5 eggs.

Nesting Location

Cooper's Hawk

Accipiter cooperii

Size Identification

Foot: Anisodactyl

Egg: Actual Size

Observation Calendar

J F M A M J J A S O N D

Male/Female: In flight: White chest and belly with rust banding down to lower belly; buff tail is long and rounded with faint charcoal banding; chin white; buff and white under wings with charcoal banding; grey on top of head. When in flight it has a steady wingbeat. **Perched**: Grey wings and tail with rust edging at ends; eyes are brick red; bill black and yellow; feet and legs yellow with rust feathers banded white down to knee.

Voice: Call is a loud **kek kek kek**.
Food: Small birds.
Nest/Eggs: Large nest built of sticks and twigs, in conifer tree, 6-18 metres above ground. 4-5 eggs.

Nesting Location

109

Northern Goshawk

Accipiter gentilis

Size Identification

Foot: Anisodactyl

Egg: 80%

Observation Calendar

J F M A M J J A S O N D

Male/Female: In flight: Underside is grey with dark brown banding overall; tail long with rich red along edges; buff eyebrow runs to back of neck. **Perched**: Dark brown wings with buff edging; eye brick red; bill black with yellow at base; feet and legs yellow with white feathers, banded brown reaching down to knees.

Did you know? This is an aggressive bird that has the ability to fly in densely wooded areas chasing small birds.

Voice: Loud **keeek keeek keeek**.
Food: Small birds and occasional small mammals, such as squirrels.
Nest/Eggs: Stick nest lodged in crotch of tree against the trunk, lined with bark, feathers and down. 3-4 eggs.

Nesting Location

Red-shouldered Hawk

Buteo lineatus

Observation Calendar

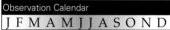
J F M A M J J A S O N D

Male/Female: In flight: Rust-red chest lightly banded with buff; pale crescent on outer area of wings. **Perched**: Red brick shoulder patch; black wings with streaks of white; head buff with dark brown streaking; tail dark with white banding; bill black with yellow at base; feet and legs yellow with buff feathers banded with rust that reach just above feet; eyes dark.

Did you know? Red-shouldered Hawks return to the same nesting site year after year.

Voice: Decreasing scream **ke-er-ke-er-ke-er.**
Food: Amphibians, snakes, small mammals, small birds, insects.
Nest/Eggs: Sticks and twigs lined with bark, feathers and down, built close to trunk in cavity of tree, near swamps and bogs. 3 eggs.

Broad-winged Hawk
Buteo platypterus

Size Identification

Foot: Anisodactyl

Egg: 75%

Observation Calendar

J F M A M J J A S O N D

Male/Female: In flight: Brownish-red banding on chest and belly; wings white with faint banding; tail broad with large black banding against white; chin white; top of head brown. **Perched**: Dark brown wings; yellow eye ringed in black; feet and legs yellow; bill charcoal grey.

Did you know? In September hawks sometimes gather together in flocks of hundreds.

Voice: Whistle that is high-pitched **peee peeeeee**.
Food: Small mammals, birds, reptiles, amphibians.
Nest/Eggs: Small stick, twigs and leaves, lined with bark, in main supporting branches of tree, against trunk. 2-3 eggs.

Nesting Location

Red-tailed Hawk

Buteo jamaicensis

Size Identification

Foot: Anisodactyl

Egg: 75%

Observation Calendar

J F M A M J J A S O N D

Male/Female: In flight: Tail will appear faint red depending on light; broad wings and belly, white banded with charcoal. **Perched**: Wings are dark brown with buff edges; eyes brick red; bill yellow and black; feet and legs yellow with white feathers banded brown/charcoal reaching to knees; tail brick red.

Voice: A scream that is downward **keeer er er.**
Food: Small mammals, amphibians, nestlings, insects, reptiles, birds.
Nest/Eggs: Flat and shallow, stick and twig nest, lined with moss and evergreen sprigs, on rocky ledges or in trees that are in the open, 10-30 metres above ground. 2 eggs.

Nesting Location

Rough-legged Hawk

Buteo lagopus

Size Identification

Foot: Anisodactyl

Observation Calendar

J F M A M J J A S O N D

Male/Female: In flight: Dark patches on white belly with banding; black patch at wrist of underwing; white tail with one dark band at tip. **Perched:** Dark brown wings with buff head that is banded with dark brown; yellow eyes; base of tail white rump; black bill, yellow at base; yellow feet and legs with buff feathers that are banded brown to knees.

Food: Small rodents.
Voice: A whistle along with a **keeeerrr** that descends.
Nest/Eggs: Stick nest in tree. 2-4 eggs

Nesting Location

Golden Eagle

Aquila chrysaetos

Size Identification

Foot: Anisodactyl

Observation Calendar

J F M A M J J A S O N D

Male/Female: Large eagle; warm golden-brown overall; yellow bill darker at tip; yellow feet and legs; very broad dark wings; head extends far out from wing base. **In flight**: Wings slightly V-shaped. Immature has white at base of primaries and tail.

Food: Small mammals such as rabbits and rodents. Occasionally birds such as ducks and geese.
Voice: Chirps repeatedly near food, otherwise quiet.

Nesting Location

American Kestrel
Falco sparverius

Size Identification

Foot: Anisodactyl

Egg: Actual Size

Observation Calendar
J F M A M J J A S O N D

Male/Female: In flight: Overall buff with black speckles; distinctive black banding on face. **Perched**: charcoal wings with black, separated banding; back rust with black banding; grey top of head with rust patch on top; black bands running down cheeks against white; bill black / charcoal with yellow at base; feet and legs orange; tail deep rust with broad black tip.

Voice: Rapid **klee klee klee** or **kily kily kily.**
Food: Mice, voles, insects, small birds.
Nest/Eggs: In cavity of tree or man-made boxes, little or no nesting material. 3-5 eggs.

Nesting Location

Merlin

Falco columbarius

Size Identification

Foot: Anisodactyl

Egg: Actual Size

Observation Calendar

J F M A M J J A S O N D

Male: In flight: Buff underside with dark brown banding overall; dark brown head with thin buff eyebrow; tail dark.
Perched: Slate-blue wings with slight amount of white edges; bill black with yellow at base; feet and legs pale yellow.
Female: Brown back and wings; buff underparts with brown streaks.

Did you know? Often called the "bullet hawk," this is a very fast bird when racing after its prey. It has a wonderful ability to turn quickly and accelerate in flight, even through thick woods.

Voice: Rapid and high-pitched **clee clee clee.**
Food: Small birds in flight, reptiles, amphibians, insects.
Nest/Eggs: Sticks interwoven with moss, twigs, lichen and conifer needles, on cliff ledge or cavity of tree. 4-5 eggs.

Nesting Location

Peregrine Falcon

Falco peregrinus

Size Identification

Foot: Anisodactyl

Egg: 80%

Observation Calendar

J F M A M J J A S O N D

Male/Female: In flight: Overall white underside with charcoal banding; face has black mask and sideburns with yellow around dark eyes; bill is yellow and grey' feet and legs are yellow.
Perched: Black wings with buff edging on feathers.

Did you know? The Peregrine can reach the fastest speeds of any animal on earth — 260 km/h.

Voice: A series of high pitched screams **ki ki ki.**
Food: Catches birds in flight and occasionally will eat larger insects.
Nest/Eggs: Slight hollow in rock ledge or flat roof top, built with sticks. 3-5 eggs.

Nesting Location

Ring-necked Pheasant

Phasianus colchicus

Foot: Anisodactyl

Egg: 90%

Observation Calendar

J F M A M J J A S O N D

Male: Green iridescent head with distinctive red wattles (patches around eye); white collar; overall body is mixture of grey, black and brown; long tail feathers brown with black banding; feet and legs charcoal grey; pale yellow bill.
Female: Grey-brown overall with dark markers over entire body; pale yellow bill; small red wattle above eye.

Did you know? This chicken-like bird gets into some real cock fights in early spring, jumping, pecking, clawing for its right to territory.

Voice: Similar to a wild turkey gobble at a higher pitch.
Food: Seeds, insects, grains, berries.
Nest/Eggs: Shallow bowl on ground, lined with weed, grass and leaves. 6-15 eggs.

Nesting Location

119

Ruffed Grouse

Bonasa umbellus

Observation Calendar

J F M A M J J A S O N D

Male: Distinctive crest on head; overall brown speckled bird with black shoulder band on back of neck; tail is grey with broad black band at tip; eye brown; feet and legs grey.
Female: Similar to male except browner and more barring on underside; black shoulder band is narrower.

Did you know? The female will act injured if there is a threat near the nest.

Voice: An alarm note of **qit qit**. Cooing by female.
Food: A variety of insects, seeds, tree buds, leaves and berries.
Nest/Eggs: Hollow under log or near the base of a tree, lined with leaves, pine needles and feathers. 9-12 eggs.

Wild Turkey

Meleagris gallopavo

Size Identification

Foot: Anisodactyl

Egg: 65%

Observation Calendar

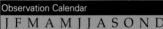

J F M A M J J A S O N D

Male: An extremely large bird; overall dark dusky-brown body; iridescent bronze sheen and banding of reddish-brown, black and white; head is featherless, grey and red; blueish and reddish wattles; tail is fan shaped when open and has chestnut or buff tips; spurs and 'beard' on breast; feet and legs reddish-grey.

Female: Smaller than male and less iridescence; no spurs or 'beard.'

Voice: Gobbling and clucking calls.

Food: Seeds, grains, insects, frogs, lizards, vegetation, nuts.

Nest/Eggs: Scraped depression in ground, lined with leaves and grasses. 6-20 eggs.

Nesting Location

Rock Pigeon

Size Identification

Size Identification

Foot: Anisodactyl

Egg: Actual Size

Observation Calendar

J F M A M J J A S O N D

Male/Female: Varies greatly from solid white to solid black and everything in between. Most birds have dark grey head with hints of iridescent colours along the neck; body light grey with two charcoal wing bands; tail and wings dark grey with black bands; rump is white.

Did you know? Pigeons were introduced to North America in the 1800s. They are now prevalent everywhere, especially in urban areas.

Voice: Soft descending **kooooo kooooo.**
Food: Seeds and grain
Nest/Eggs: Flimsy nest of twigs, grass, straw and debris, on ledges or crevices of buildings and bridges, in colonies. 1-2 eggs.

Nesting Location

Mourning Dove

Zenaida macroura

Size Identification

Foot: Anisodactyl

Egg: Actual Size

Backyard Feeder

Nesting Location

Observation Calendar

J F M A M J J A S O N D

Male: Buff-coloured head and body; dark grey wings and tail; bill is black with speckles of red at opening; wings have small black feathers highlighted against softer grey; eyes black surrounded by light blue; feet and legs red; tail is long and pointed.
Female: Similar except head, neck and chest are evenly brown.

Did you know? When the mourning dove is in flight its wings whistle.

Voice: Very distinct cooing that sounds a little sad, **coooahooo oo oo oo** fading at the end.
Food: A variety of seeds and grain.
Nest/Eggs: Platform of sticks and twigs, lined with grass and rootlets, in evergreens, 15 metres above ground. 1-2 eggs.

Black-billed Cuckoo
Coccyzus erythropthalmus

Size Identification

Foot: Anisodactyl

Egg: Actual Size

Observation Calendar
J F M A M J J A S O N D

Male/Female: Distinct black beak curved slightly downward; red ring around black eyes; upper body parts brown; wings brown; long tail with three white spots on underside; white chin, chest and belly; feet and legs charcoal grey.

Did you know? The Black-billed Cuckoo is an important species for farmers since much of its diet consists of caterpillars, which are destructive to plants.

Voice: Softly repeated **cu cu cu cu cu** in groups of two to five at the same pitch.
Food: Insects, lizards, mollusks, fishes, frogs, berries.
Nest/Eggs: Shallow, built of twigs and grasses and lined with softer materials including ferns, roots and plant-down; usually built near tree trunk in dense area. 2-5 eggs.

Nesting Location

Common Barn Owl

Tyto alba

Foot: Zygodactyl

Egg: Actual Size

Observation Calendar

J F M A M J J A S O N D

Male/Female: Large heart-shaped white face with reddish-brown trim; overall reddish-brown, light brown and black mottled; neck, chest and belly white with dark streaking; long legs covered in white feathers; feet yellow.

Did you know? The Common Barn Owl has the most acute hearing of all the owls. In total darkness it can hear mouse footsteps within a 30-metre area. Despite its name, this bird is extremely rare.

Voice: Hissing and screeching sounds with occasional clicks. Mostly quiet unless approached.
Food: Rats, mice, insects, bats, various reptiles.
Nest/Eggs: Cavity nest built in old barns or buildings, or in holes already established by mammals along cliffs or banks. No nest materials. 4-7 eggs.

Birdhouse Nester

Nesting Location

Eastern Screech Owl

Otus asio

Size Identification

Foot: Zygodactyl

Egg: Actual Size

Observation Calendar

J F M A M J J A S O N D

Male/Female: Small owl overall with reddish or grey morphs; large yellow eyes; feet and legs yellow; white chest with dark brown streaking; small ear tufts.

Voice: Ascending winnows or melodic trill at same pitch.
Food: Small mammals, insects, amphibians, small birds.
Nest/Eggs: Cavity nest with no linings. 3-5 eggs.

Birdhouse Nester

Nesting Location

Great Horned Owl

Bubo virginianus

Size Identification

Foot: Zygodactyl

Observation Calendar

J F M A M J J A S O N D

Egg: 80%

Male/Female: Very recognizable ear tufts that sit wide apart; bright yellow eyes surrounded by rust colour; grey and brown overall with black bands.

Voice: Hoot consists of several **hoo hoo hoo hoo hoo hoo**. Male is deeper then female.
Food: Small mammals, birds, reptiles.
Nest/Eggs: Nests in a deserted hawk's, heron's or crow's nest with very little material added. Occasionally will lay eggs on ground amongst bones, skulls and bits of fur. 1-3 eggs.

Nesting Location

Snowy Owl
Nyctea scandiaca

Size Identification

Foot: Zygodactyl

Observation Calendar

J F M A M J J A S O N D

Male/Female: Short black bill; overall white with brilliant yellow eye; small amount of grey speckling throughout with very faint grey banding on chest and sides; feet are covered in white feathers, with long black claws.

Voice: High-pitched screech in breeding and low muffled hoot repeated.
Food: Small mammals, fish, birds, carrion.
Nest/Eggs: Slight depression on ground lined with moss and grass. 5-7 eggs.

Nesting Location

Barred Owl

Strix varia

Size Identification

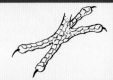

Foot: Zygodactyl

Egg: 80%

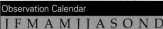

Observation Calendar

J F M A M J J A S O N D

Male/Female: Large dark eyes set in buff and rich brown; white bands extend out from face, down the back including wings and tail feathers; chest white with rich brown feathers in columns; bill is small, yellow, hook shape.

Did you know? The Barred Owl's ears are positioned differently on either side of the head. This allows for better hearing in total darkness.

Voice: Very rhythmic hoots in series of four or five at a time.
Food: Small mammals
Nest/Eggs: Cavity of tree or abandoned hawk's or crow's nest; no lining added. 2-3 eggs.

Nesting Location

Long-eared Owl
Asio otus

Size Identification

Foot: Zygodactyl

Egg: Actual Size

Observation Calendar

J F M A M J J A S O N D

Male/Female: Overall brown mottled with buff; large yellow eyes surrounded by dark areas; cup on face with white rim; short curved black bill; legs covered in white feathers; feet yellow; light belly with subtle streaking on sides; tufts rarely seen.

Did you know? The Long-eared Owl will live in a small community of other owls during the winter months.

Food: Small mammals but favouring voles. Young owls will hunt songbirds and other game birds.
Voice: Low **hooooo** in a long series of notes. Snarls and squeals if approached during feeding.
Nest/Eggs: Nest in trees 3-10 metres above ground. They will usually use the old nest of a crow, hawk or squirrel.
3-7 eggs.

Nesting Location

Short-eared Owl

Asio flammeus

Size Identification

Foot: Zygodactyl

Egg: 70%

Observation Calendar

J F M A M J J A S O N D

Male/Female: Dark brown overall with buff banding on back; small ear tufts black and buff directly above eyes on top of head (rarely seen); wings and tail feathers dark brown with buff bands; light buff chest and belly with brown streaks; long wings tipped black at the ends; eyes brilliant yellow surrounded by black; bill black; feet and legs black.

Did you know? The Short-eared Owl flies low to the ground when hunting but is able to hover momentarily when prey is spotted.

Voice: Raspy **yip yip yip.**

Food: Small mammals, mostly voles, songbirds and game birds.

Nest/Eggs: Slight depression hidden in grass. Lined with grass and feathers. 4-9 eggs.

Nesting Location

Northern Saw-whet Owl

Aegolius acadicus

Size Identification

Foot: Zygodactyl

Egg: Actual Size

Observation Calendar
J F M A M J J A S O N D

Male/Female: Yellow eyes that are surrounded by a reddish-brown facial disk; chest white with brown streaks running length of body; feet and legs grey.

Voice: Whistled song repeated **too too too.**
Food: Diet consists mainly of small mammals, including voles, chipmunks and bats, also insects.
Nest/Eggs: Cavity of dead tree, 4-18 metres above ground. No material added. 2-6 eggs.

Nesting Location

Common Nighthawk

Chordeiles minor

Size Identification

Foot: Anisodactyl

Egg: Actual Size

Observation Calendar

J F M A M J J A S O N D

Male: Grey and black speckled bird with long thin wings; white collar wraps around to bottom of neck; legs and feet light grey. When in flight white bands near tail are visible.

Did you know? This bird eats in flight by scooping insects into its large mouth. You can often see nighthawks feeding near lights on warm nights.

Voice: A nasal sounding *peeent*.
Food: Flying insects.
Nest/Eggs: In depression on the ground, often in gravel, with lining. 2 eggs.

Nesting Location

Whip-poor-will

Caprimulgus vociferus

Size Identification

Foot: Anisodactyl

Egg: Actual Size

Observation Calendar

J F M A M J J A S O N D

Male/Female: Grey fluffy bird with brown cheeks; short black rounded wings; short tail; black bill lightly covered with feathers; large black eyes.

Voice: A series of *whip-poor-will, whip-poor-will* with accent on last word.

Food: Flying insects including moths, beetles and grasshoppers.

Nest/Eggs: Depression of dead leaves on the ground formed around eggs. 2 eggs.

Nesting Location

Chimney Swift

Chaetura pelagica

Size Identification

Foot: Anisodactyl

Egg: Actual Size

Observation Calendar

J F M A M J J A S O N D

Male/Female: Dark charcoal on head, back, wings and tail; lighter on chest and throat; black bill is small with light grey on underside; feet and legs grey.

Did you know? A Chimney Swift is capable of snapping off tree twigs with its feet while in flight. It then takes the twig in its mouth and returns to its nest.

Voice: A very quick and repeated *chitter, chitter, chitter* with occasional *chip.*
Food: Flying insects such as moths and beetles.
Nest/Eggs: Flimsy half cup attached by saliva to crevice or rock ledge in chimneys, barns, old buildings and on rock formations. 3-6 eggs.

Nesting Location

Ruby-throated Hummingbird

Archilochus colubris

Observation Calendar

J F M A M J J A S O N D

Male: Dark green head which is iridescent in parts; red throat begins darker under chin; white collar, breast and belly; wings and notched tail black; iridescent green on back; black bill is long and thin; small white area behind eyes; feet and legs black.
Female: Head, back and parts of tail are bright iridescent green; white throat, chest and belly; wings and tail black with white outer tips; black bill is long and thin; small white area behind eyes; feet and legs black.

Voice: A low *hummmmmm* followed occasionally by an angry sounding squeak or chattering.
Food: Nectar from a variety of plants including thistles, jewel-weed, trumpet vines and other blossoms, occasionally insects.
Nest/Eggs: Small, tightly woven cup with deep cavity built with fibres and attached with spider web, lined with plant down, covered on the outside with lichens, in tree or shrub, 3-6 metres above ground. 2 eggs.

136

Belted Kingfisher

Ceryle alcyon

Size Identification

Foot: Anisodactyl

Egg: Actual Size

Observation Calendar

J F M A M J J A S O N D

Male: A large head and long black bill; crested blue/black head; very short blue tail; wings black with white bands; chest white; white collar wraps around neck with blue band that wraps around chest; feet and legs charcoal.
Female: Same as male except a rust-coloured breast band.

Did you know? Belted Kingfishers teach their young to dive for food by catching a fish, stunning it, then placing it on the surface of the water. The young birds then practise diving for it.

Voice: A continuous deep rattle during flight.
Food: Small fish, amphibians, reptiles, insects, crayfish.
Nest/Eggs: A cavity or tunnel excavated in a bank near a river or lake. 5-8 eggs.

Nesting Location

Size Identification

Foot: Zygodactyl

Egg: Actual Size

Backyard Feeder

Nesting Location

Red-headed Woodpecker

Melanerpes erythrocephalus

Observation Calendar

J F M A M J J A S O N D

Male/Female: Bright red hood over head with grey and black bill; back is black with large distinctive white patches on wings; feet and legs grey; tail feathers are pointed and black; chest and belly white.

Did you know? These woodpeckers are declining because of forestry practices and are competing unsuccessfully with European starlings for nesting locations.

Voice: Call is a deep hoarse *queer queeeer queeer*.
Food: A variety of insects and insect larvae.
Nest/Eggs: Cavity of tree with no added material, 2-25 metres above ground. 4-7 eggs.

Red-bellied Woodpecker

Melanerpes carolinus

Male: Bright red cap stretching down back of neck; long sharp

Size Identification

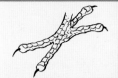

Foot: Zygodactyl

Egg: Actual Size

Observation Calendar

J F M A M J J A S O N D

black beak; tan chin, chest and belly; short black tail with white stripes; black back with white bands; feet and legs charcoal grey; reddish patch on lower belly seldom visible.
Female: Grey face with red crown running down back of head.

Did you know? The Red-bellied Woodpecker will store food in tree cavities and crevices.

Voice: Harsh *churrrr* and *chuck chuck chuck* descending in pitch. Drums and bursts.
Food: Insects, fruit, seeds, nuts.
Nest/Eggs: Creates cavity in living or nearly dead tree. 3-8 eggs.

Backyard Feeder

Birdhouse Nester

Nesting Location

Size Identification

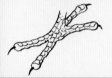

Foot: Zygodactyl

Egg: Actual Size

Backyard Feeder

Nesting Location

Yellow-bellied Sapsucker

Sphyrapicus varius

Observation Calendar
J F M A M J J A S O N D

Male: Red cap and chin with black outlines; white face with black line running through eye from bill to back of head; centre of belly yellow; feet and legs black.
Female: Chin white, not red.

Voice: Drumming on trees in quick short bursts followed by irregular drumming. Occasional *chuurrrr* or *weep*.
Food: Flying insects, spiders, berries, fruit. Drinks sap from trees.
Nest/Eggs: Cavity builder, often in decaying aspens or other trees. 5-6 eggs.

Downy Woodpecker

Picoides pubescens

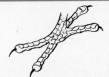

Size Identification

Foot: Zygodactyl

Observation Calendar

J F M A M J J A S O N D

Male: Black crown ends in very bright red spot on back of head; white extends from cheeks to lower belly; wings and tail black with white banding; feet and legs grey.
Female: Similar except without red spot on back of head.

Voice: Whiny call and a *queek queek* call during courtship. Listen for bird pounding on trees looking for insects.
Food: Larvae and other tree-dwelling insects.
Nest/Eggs: Cavity for nest excavated in decaying trees, 1-5 metres above ground. 3-6 eggs.

Egg: Actual Size

Backyard Feeder

Nesting Location

141

Hairy Woodpecker

Picoides villosus

Foot: Zygodactyl

Egg: Actual Size

Backyard Feeder

Nesting Location

Observation Calendar
J F M A M J J A S O N D

Male/Female: Black head with white banding along cheek and through eye; white back and underparts; wings and tail black with white spotting; feet and legs charcoal grey; bill is nearly length of head; outer tail feathers white.

Voice: A bright sounding , which may be followed by a rattling call. call during courtship.

Food: Larvae, wood-boring insects. At feeders suet and wildflower seeds.

Nest/Eggs: Cavity for nest excavated in live trees, 1-5 metres above ground. 4-6 eggs.

Northern Flicker

Colaptes auratus

Size Identification

Foot: Zygodactyl

Egg: Actual Size

Backyard Feeder

Nesting Location

Observation Calendar

J F M A M J J A S O N D

Male: Grey at top of head which stops at bright red spot on back of neck; black eye is encircled in light brown, with a black line running off bill to lower neck; chest begins with black half-moon necklace on front and turns into a white belly with black spots; wings and tail greyish-brown with black banding; white rump; yellow feathers are evident under sharp pointed tail feathers while in flight.

Female: Similar to male except without the black line running from bill.

Voice: Various sounds depending on its use. When claiming its territory a series of *kekekekeke* and when in courtship *woeka-woeka-woeka*.

Food: Digs and pokes on the ground looking for ants and other insects, fruit and seeds. Most of its diet consists of ants.

Nest/Eggs: Cavity of tree with no added material, .5-18 metres above ground. 3-10 eggs.

Pileated Woodpecker

Dryocopus pileatus

Size Identification

Foot: Zygodactyl

Egg: Actual Size

Backyard Feeder

Nesting Location

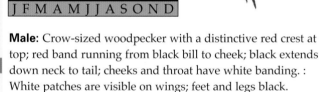

Observation Calendar
J F M A M J J A S O N D

Male: Crow-sized woodpecker with a distinctive red crest at top; red band running from black bill to cheek; black extends down neck to tail; cheeks and throat have white banding. : White patches are visible on wings; feet and legs black.
Female: Black forehead replaces portion of red crest. No red band from bill to cheek.

Did you know? The Pileated Woodpecker can be so aggressive when chiseling away at trees that it can weaken the tree to falling point.

Voice: A quick set of calls, in duets, sometimes followed by a sharp when contacting mate.
Food: Larvae, ants and tree-dwelling insects, wild fruits, acorns, beechnuts.
Nest/Eggs: Cavity of tree with no added material. 3-4 eggs.

144

Olive-sided Flycatcher

Contopus cooperi

Size Identification

Foot: Anisodactyl

Observation Calendar

J F M A M J J A S O N D

Egg: Actual Size

Male/Female: Dark grey/olive overall with crest at back of head; bar of white that runs down front from under chin to lower belly; white tufts on sides of rump but could be hidden by wings; feet and legs black; bill black on top with yellow underside.

Voice: A loud whistled hick, *three-bee-er* with first word quieter than others and the second accented. A warning *chirp pip pip pip*.
Food: Flying insects.
Nest/Eggs: Flat cup attached to horizontal branch of conifer tree or shrub built with twigs, small roots and lichens and lined with pine needles and small roots, 2-15 metres above ground. 3 eggs.

Nesting Location

Eastern Wood-Pewee
Contopus virens

Size Identification

Foot: Anisodactyl

Observation Calendar
J F M A M J J A S O N D

Egg: Actual Size

Male/Female: Olive-grey overall with head that is crested at back; wings black and dark grey with two white bars; throat and chest white; belly slightly yellow or white; tail charcoal; bill black on top and yellow underside; feet and legs black.

Did you know? The Wood-Pewee changes its voice in morning and evening, converting its song into a slow verse.

Voice: A soft whistle *pee-a-wee pee-awee* repeated without any pause early in the morning.
Food: Flies, beetles, bees, ants and other insects.
Nest/Eggs: Shallow cup built with grass, spider's web and fibres, lined with hair, covered outside with lichens, on horizontal branch of tree far out from trunk, 5-20 metres above ground. 3-5 eggs.

Nesting Location

Yellow-bellied Flycatcher

Empidonax flaviventris

Observation Calendar
J F M A M J J A S O N D

Male: Olive-green head, back, wings and tail feathers; yellowish throat and breast; wings have two yellow bands; black eye has yellow ring; feet and legs black; thin bill is dark grey on top with yellow underside or it can be all dark.

Voice: A simple and sweet *pu-wee peawee*.
Food: Flying insects.
Nest/Eggs: Deep cup built with mosses and lined with black rootlets, pine needles, grass and moss, on or near ground, at base of conifer tree. 3-4 eggs.

Willow Flycatcher

Empidonax traillii

Size Identification

Foot: Anisodactyl

Egg: Actual Size

Observation Calendar

J F M A M J J A S O N D

Male/Female: Olive-brown upperparts; white throat; chest and belly tinted yellow; feet and legs black; two rows of white banding on wings; faint eye ring.

Food: Flying insects.
Voice: Song is accented on the first note. Song is *Fitsbyou*. Call is *wit*.
Nest/Eggs: Cup-shaped nest built from and lined with plant fibres. 3-4 eggs.

Nesting Location

Least Flycatcher

Empidonax minimus

Foot: Anisodactyl

Egg: Actual Size

Observation Calendar

J F M A M J J A S O N D

Male/Female: Smallest of the flycatchers with a brown/olive head and back; rump is slightly golden; throat white and washes to a grey breast and a pale yellow belly; black eye is ringed with white; wings dark brown and black with white wing bands; tail dark olive/brown with white edges.

Did you know? The Least Flycatcher is not afraid of humans and in pursuit of a flying insect will dive within inches of a person.

Voice: Song is *chibic chibic chibic* repeated with accent in middle of phrase.
Food: Flying insects.
Nest/Eggs: Compact and deep cup built with bark, weeds, grasses and lined with thistle, feathers, hair and fibres, in upright fork of tree or shrub, 1-20 metres above ground. 3-6 eggs.

Nesting Location

Eastern Phoebe
Sayornis phoebe

Size Identification

Foot: Anisodactyl

Egg: Actual Size

Observation Calendar
J F M A M J J A S O N D

Male/Female: Grey-brown head and back with white throat, chest and belly; feet and legs black; white wing bands; pale yellow belly.

Did you know? One quick way to identify this bird is to watch the greyish brown tail bobbing up and down.

Voice: Song is rough sounding *fee bee fee bee.* Call is *wit.*
Food: Flying insects as well as ground insects.
Nest/Eggs: Large shelf structure built with weeds, grass, fibres and mud, covered with moss, lined with grass and hair. 3-6 eggs. Often nests in building eavestroughing.

Nesting Location

GreatCrestedFlycatcher

Myiarchus crinitus

Size Identification

Foot: Anisodactyl

Egg: Actual Size

Observation Calendar
J F M A M J J A S O N D

Male/Female: Olive/grey head with crest; back is olive/grey; wings are black with olive/grey edges and rust colour on outer edge; tail strong reddish-brown; throat soft grey changing to pale yellow at belly; feet and legs black.

Did you know? The Great Crested Flycatcher will sometimes use foil or cellophane in its nest because it is attracted to reflective objects.

Voice: A throaty whistle *wheeep* or a rolling *prrrreeeet*.
Food: Flying insects and a variety of ground insects.
Nest/Eggs: Bulky cup built with twig, leaves, feather, bark and cast off snakeskin, or Cellophane, in natural cavity of tree, up to 18 metres above ground. 4-8 eggs.

Birdhouse Nester

Nesting Location

Eastern Kingbird
Tyrannus tyrannus

Observation Calendar
J F M A M J J A S O N D

Male/Female: Black head, back, wings and tail; white chin, chest and belly; wings have white along edge and tail has white band along tip; feet and legs black.

Did you know? Size does not matter to the Eastern Kingbird: it will attack crows, ravens, hawks and owls to defend its territory.

Voice: Several different calls including *tzi tzee* as a true song. Also a *kitter kitter kitter* when threatened.
Food: Flying insects and fruit in late summer.
Nest/Eggs: Bulky cup built with weed stalks, grass and moss, in branches of tree or shrub, 3-6 metres above ground. 3-5 eggs.

Loggerhead Shrike

Lanius ludovicianus

Size Identification

Foot: Anisodactyl

Egg: Actual Size

Observation Calendar

J F M A M J J A S O N D

Male/Female: Grey overall body; distinct black mask; short black bill slightly curved at tip; chin, chest and belly grey; tail feathers black with white edges; feet and legs black.

Did you know? The Loggerhead Shrike stores freshly caught food by impaling it on thorns.

Voice: Call is *chak chak* along with a series of whistles.
Food: Small mammals, insects, small birds.
Nest/Eggs: Cuplike nest built of twigs and mosses, in tree or bush. 4-6 eggs.

Nesting Location

Size Identification

Foot: Anisodactyl

Northern Shrike

Lanius excubitor

Observation Calendar

J F M A M J J A S O N D

Male/Female: Black mask that may be dull at times; long sharp hooked black bill; head and back grey; throat, chest and belly soft grey with light grey banding from chest to lower belly; feet and legs black; wings and tail black with white edges.

Did you know? This bird is more like a hawk or owl because of its diet and hunting technique. Once the Northern Shrike has caught its prey it will often hang it in a thorny bush, saving it for later.

Voice: A light song along with
Food: Small birds and mammals, but diet consists mainly of grasshoppers, locust, crickets and other large insects.
Nest/Eggs: Bulky woven cup built with sticks, twigs, grass and small roots, lined with cotton, feather and bark, in tree or shrub, up to 10 metres above ground. 4-7 eggs.

Nesting Location

Blue-headed Vireo

Vireo solitarius

Size Identification

Foot: Anisodactyl

Egg: Actual Size

Nesting Location

Observation Calendar

J F M A M J J A S O N D

Male/Female: Blue-grey head and back with shades of olive along back; eye is brown with distinctive white eyebrow encircling it; bill long and black; feet and legs charcoal; throat and belly white with olive along edges of belly; tail charcoal with white edges.

Did you know? Although these birds are not common in parks, they are very tame when approached. Sometimes they will continue to sit on their nest even in the presence of humans, while other birds would probably attack or retreat from the area with a few choice tweeeeps.

Voice: The song is a series of short whistled phrases interrupted by pauses, similar to the Red-eyed Vireo but higher pitched and sweeter.
Food: Small insects, fruit.
Nest/Eggs: Suspended basketlike cup built with bark, fibre, grass, small roots and hair in a tree, 1-6 metres above ground. 3-5 eggs.

Warbling Vireo

Vireo gilvus

Size Identification

Foot: Anisodactyl

Egg: Actual Size

Observation Calendar

J F M A M J J A S O N D

Male/Female: Grey and green head, neck and back; white eyebrow extending from black bill; white chin, breast and belly with variable amounts of yellow; feet and legs black; tail and wings black with white edging.

Voice: The best way to find a Warbling Vireo is to listen. This bird sings throughout the day with a beautiful warbling sound. Song is a group of slurred phrases such as *brig-a-dier brig-a-dier brigate.*

Food: Small insects including caterpillars, beetles and moths, some berries.

Nest/Eggs: Tightly woven pensile cup built with bark, leaves, grass, feathers, plant down and spider's web, lined with stems and horsehair, suspended in tall trees at the edge of wooded area, well away from trunk. 3-5 eggs.

Nesting Location

Red-eyed Vireo

Vireo olivaceus

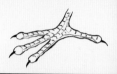

Observation Calendar

J F M A M J J A S O N D

Male/Female: red eye encircled with thin line of black set against a wide white eyebrow that runs from bill to back of head; black bill; throat and chest white; feet and legs black; back and rump are olive green; wings and tail black with edges of olive green; eye is darker brown in winter.

Voice: The Red-eyed Vireo may sound over 40 different phrases in just 60 seconds, then begin all over again. A variety of short phrases, which include .

Food: Small insects, berries, fruit.

Nest/Eggs: Deep cup built with grass, paper, bark, rootlets, vine and decorated outside with spider's web and lichen, suspended in branches, .5-18 metres above ground. 2 eggs.

Blue Jay

Cyanocitta cristata

Size Identification

Size Identification

Foot: Anisodactyl

Egg: Actual Size

Backyard Feeder

Observation Calendar
J F M A M J J A S O N D

Male/Female: Bright blue crested head with black band running through eye to just under crest on back of neck; black band continues along side of neck on both sides to chest; white under chin; back is blue; wings and tail are blue banded with black and tipped with white at ends; black bill is large with light feathers covering nostril area; feet and legs black.

Did you know? The Blue Jay has a bad reputation for eating eggs of other birds, and even their young.

Voice: Call is *jay jay jay*, plus many other calls including mimicking hawks.
Food: Omnivorous — in summer months the Blue Jay feasts on just about anything, including spiders, snails, salamanders, frogs, seeds and caterpillars. In winter months it supplements its diet with acorns and other nuts stored in tree cavities earlier in the year.
Nest/Eggs: Bulky nest of sticks, leaves, string and moss, lined with small roots, well hidden, 1-15 metres above ground, in tree or shrub. 3-4 eggs.

Nesting Location

American Crow

Foot: Anisodactyl

Observation Calendar

J F M A M J J A S O N D

Male/Female: Overall shiny black with a hint of purple in direct sunlight; large broad black bill; short and slightly square tail; feet and legs black.

Egg: Actual Size

Did you know? Although one might think that crows are a nuisance, they actually devour large quantities of grasshoppers, beetles and grubs that can be destructive to crops.

Voice: A variety of calls. Most common is the long *caaaaaw* which softens at the end.

Backyard Feeder

Food: Omnivorous — insects, food waste, grains, seeds and carrion.

Nest/Eggs: Large basket of twigs, sticks, vines, moss, feathers, fur and hair, on ledge in crotch of tree or shrub. 3-4 eggs.

Nesting Location

Common Raven
Corvus corax

Size Identification

Foot: Anisodactyl

Egg: 80%

Observation Calendar
J F M A M J J A S O N D

Male/Female: Shiny, black bird overall with a blue tint; feet and legs black; black bill is long and wide and has been described as a "Roman nose"; rounded tail.

Voice: Variety of calls including buzzing, croaks and gulps.
Food: A variety of insects, carrion, small mammals and food waste.
Nest/Eggs: Large basket of twigs, sticks, vines, hair and moss, lined with animal hair, on ledge, in tree or shrub. 3-4 eggs.

Nesting Location

Horned Lark
Eremophila alpestris

Foot: Anisodactyl

Egg: Actual Size

Observation Calendar
J F M A M J J A S O N D

Male/Female: Dull brown on top; chest and belly white; wings and tail brown and black; distinctive black facial marks which include small horns (feathers) on either side of its head; chin pale yellow with black band above running through eye and down; feet and legs black.

Did you know? The horns are not always visible, but a quick way to identify the Horned Lark is that on the ground it walks and does not hop, like most small birds.

Voice: Soft twittering *tsee titi* or *zzeeet*.
Food: A variety of insects, seeds and grains.
Nest/Eggs: Hollow in ground under grass tuft, made of stems and leaves, lined with grass. 3-5 eggs.

Nesting Location

Purple Martin

Progne subis

Size Identification

Foot: Anisodactyl

Egg: Actual Size

Observation Calendar

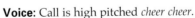

J F M A M J J A S O N D

Male: Very shiny, dark purple overall, with black wings and tail; black bill is short and slightly curved; feet and legs reddish, black; wings very long reaching to tip of tail when folded. **Female:** Dull purple head and back with black wings and tail; chest and chin grey; belly white with black speckles; feet and legs black.

Voice: Call is high pitched *cheer cheer.*
Food: Flying insects.
Nest/Eggs: Deep cup in cavity lined with grass and leaves, usually in large colonies. Nests in gourds and special martin houses. 3-8 eggs.

Birdhouse Nester

Nesting Location

Tree Swallow

Tachycineta bicolor

Size Identification

Foot: Anisodactyl

Egg: Actual Size

Observation Calendar
J F M A M J J A S O N D

Male/Female: Dark iridescent blue on head, neck, back, wings and tail; bright white chin, chest and belly; black bill is short and slightly curved; wings are very long, reaching down to tip of tail when folded; feet and legs charcoal.

Did you know? The Tree Swallow is the only swallow that eats berries in the place of insects. This allows it to winter further north than its relatives.

Voice: Early morning song *wheet trit weet*, with an alarm call of *cheedeeep*.
Food: Flying insects, berries.
Nest/Eggs: Cup in cavity of tree lined with grass and feathers, usually a woodpecker's old hole. 4–6 eggs.

Birdhouse Nester

Nesting Location

Northern Rough-winged Swallow

Stelgidopteryx serripennis

Size Identification

Foot: Anisodactyl

Egg: Actual Size

Observation Calendar

J F M A M J J A S O N D

Male/Female: Greyish pale brown upper parts; pale brown chin, chest and sides; white belly; feet and legs black; short black beak; short tail.

Voice: Harsh *brrrrrt* during aggression or danger. Musical *br rrrrt* drawn out and often doubled.
Food: Insects in flight.
Nest/Eggs: Built in cavities such as tunnels, bridges, culverts and caves, lined with grass, leaves and moss. Often with swallows in crevices in cliff faces. 4-8 eggs.

Nesting Location

Bank Swallow

Riparia riparia

Size Identification

Foot: Anisodactyl

Egg: Actual Size

Observation Calendar

J F M A M J J A S O N D

Male/Female: Dirty brown overall with white front except for brown band running across chest; wings are very long, reaching down to tip of tail when folded; feet and legs grey; black bill is short and curved.

Voice: A variety of calls including *tchirrt tchirrt* and long twittering.

Food: Flying insects as well as a variety of other insects. Main diet consists of dragonflies, flies, mayflies and beetles.

Nest/Eggs: Earth tunnel lined with grass and straw, along bank of water. 4-6 eggs.

Nesting Location

165

Cliff Swallow

Petrochelidon pyrrhonota

Size Identification

Foot: Anisodactyl

Egg: Actual Size

Observation Calendar

J F M A M J J A S O N D

Male/Female: Overall black with buff rump and brick red cheeks; white patch on forehead; belly white; back has variable amounts of white streaks; feet and legs grey; tail black, square at end.

Did you know? Nest sights can be a little competitive and the birds will steal nesting grasses and twigs from each other's nests.

Voice: A long *chuuurrrr* and a deeper *nyeeew*.
Food: A variety of insects.
Nest/Eggs: Mud lined with grass, hair and feathers, under bridges, in cliffs and buildings. 3-6 eggs.

Nesting Location

166

Barn Swallow

Hirundo rustica

Foot: Anisodactyl

Observation Calendar
J F M A M J J A S O N D

Egg: Actual Size

Male: Dark blue iridescent from top of head, shoulders, down back and top of wings; chin and chest rust colour that fades to white at belly; wings are very long and extend to tips of tail, which is forked with long feathers at either end that can be seen when bird is in flight; feet and legs charcoal; black and cream bill. When bird is in flight a band of white can be seen at end of wings.
Female: Same markings but duller.

Voice: A soft twittering *kvik kvik wit wit*.
Food: A variety of insects.
Nest/Eggs: Mud and straw, lined with feathers, in buildings, under bridges, in cliffs and caves. 4-5 eggs.

Nesting Location

Black-cappedChickadee

Poecile atricapilla

Size Identification

Foot: Anisodactyl

Egg: Actual Size

Backyard Feeder

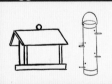

Birdhouse Nester

Nesting Location

Observation Calendar

J F M A M J J A S O N D

Male/Female: Round black head with white cheeks; black chin that contrasts against bright white bib which fades into rust on belly with buff edges; wings black and grey with white edges; tail black with white edges; feet and legs black.

Did you know? In winter Black-capped Chickadees form small flocks of about 10 birds and defend their territory from intruders.

Voice: A descending whistle with two notes and sounds like *chick-a-dee-dee-dee.*
Food: Seeds, insects, berries. Drawn to thistle-seed feeders.
Nest/Eggs: Domed cup lined with wool, hair, fur, moss and insect cocoons, in cavity of tree. 5-10 eggs.

Red-breasted Nuthatch

Sitta canadensis

Size Identification

Foot: Anisodactyl

Egg: Actual Size

Backyard Feeder

Birdhouse Nester

Nesting Location

Observation Calendar

J F M A M J J A S O N D

Male: Small round bird with black stripe over top of head and white stripe underneath running over eye to back of head, followed by another black band running through eye; white cheeks turn to rust at neck and continue rust to chest and belly; back is grey-blue; wings and tail grey becoming black at ends; black bill is often white on underside; feet and legs brown-black.
Female: Similar to male except for grey cap and light underside.

Did you know? The Red-breasted Nuthatch will smear pitch at the entrance to its nest, although it is not known why.

Voice: A tin-whistle call and an occasional loud *knack knack*.
Food: Seeds, insects, flying insects.
Nest/Eggs: Cup lined with grass, moss and feathers, in excavated cavity or crevice of tree, 1-12 metres above ground. 4-7 eggs.

White-breasted Nuthatch

Sitta carolinensis

Size Identification

Foot: Anisodactyl

Egg: Actual Size

Backyard Feeder

Birdhouse Nester

Nesting Location

Observation Calendar

J F M A M J J A S O N D

Male: Shiny black on top of head running down the back, turning to lighter blue-grey on back; face and neck white, which runs down chest and belly; slight rust colours on sides; wings and tail are blue-grey with white edges; feet and legs black.
Female: Similar to male except top of head and back are lighter grey.

Did you know? These little birds are known for their ability to run down tree trunks headfirst, at a very fast pace.

Voice: Nesting pairs keep in contact with one another with a deep sounding *aank aank* but also chatter a soft *ip ip*.
Food: Spiders, insects, seeds, insect eggs, acorns.
Nest/Eggs: Cup lined with twigs, feathers, small roots, fur and hair, in natural cavity or crevice of tree, 4-15 metres above ground. 5-10 eggs.

Brown Creeper

Certhia americana

Size Identification

Foot: Anisodactyl

Observation Calendar

J F M A M J J A S O N D

Male/Female: Overall brown with grey streaks and white chin, chest and belly; long curved bill that is black on top and white/pink on bottom; distinctive eye stripe; feet and legs grey; tail is long and pointed.

Did you know? Spending most of its day creeping up and down trees looking for meals, the Brown Creeper can flatten itself and blend into the colour of the tree trunk when a predator passes by.

Voice: A very high whistling *see wee see tu eee.*
Food: Insects, insect and spider eggs and occasionally nuts and seeds.
Nest/Eggs: Cup with foundation of twigs, bark, and leaves, lined with bark, grass, feathers and moss, in cavity or under loose bark of tree, up to 5 metres above ground. 4-8 eggs.

Backyard Feeder

Birdhouse Nester

Nesting Location

Carolina Wren

Thryothorus ludovicianus

Size Identification

Foot: Anisodactyl

Egg: Actual Size

Observation Calendar
J F M A M J J A S O N D

Male/Female: Overall brown body with warmer brown on upperparts; distinct white eyebrow; long tail with black banding; feet and legs brown; white rump.

Did you know? The Carolina Wren usually holds its tail cocked upright.

Voice: Variety of notes and trills. Song is *tea kettle, tea kettle*. Call is *chip*.
Food: Insects, spiders.
Nest/Eggs: Cavity nest built with hair, twigs and grasses and lined with feathers and soft grasses. 4-6 eggs.

Birdhouse Nester

Nesting Location

House Wren

Troglodytes aedon

Observation Calendar

J F M A M J J A S O N D

Male/Female: Brown upper parts; light buff eyebrows; short rust and black-banded tail that is often cocked; light buff chin, chest and belly; light buff banding along sides; feet and legs greyish-pink; sharp black beak with yellow lower mandible.

Voice: Warbling that descends for 2-3 seconds. Call is a variety of buzzes and rattling *chur*.
Food: Insects.
Nest/Eggs: In cavities of trees or birdhouses, twigs lined with softer material including moss, feathers, rootlets and grasses. 5-6 eggs.

Winter Wren

Troglodytes troglodytes

Size Identification

Foot: Anisodactyl

Egg: Actual Size

Observation Calendar
J F M A M J J A S O N D

Male/Female: One of the smallest wrens, with a very short tail; mixed browns on head and back with faint banding in black; wings and tail brown with black banding; feet and legs red; black bill is slightly white on underside; long talons.

Did you know? You may think you are seeing a mouse when you first spot the Winter Wren. It likes to keep near the ground and its movements are similar to a field mouse.

Voice: Call is *chip chip* with a variety of songs including twittering and twinkles.
Food: Insects, insect eggs, spiders.
Nest/Eggs: Domed cup under roots in tangled growth near ground built with weed, twig, moss, grass and lined with hair and feather. 4-7 eggs.

Nesting Location

Marsh Wren

Cistothorus palustris

Size Identification

Foot: Anisodactyl

Egg: Actual Size

Observation Calendar

J F M A M J J A S O N D

Male/Female: Overall reddish-brown; white streaks on head and back; extremely dark brown crown; white eyebrow; white throat and chest; feet and legs red.

Did you know? The male will build a number of different courting nests during mating season and will sometimes take several different mates during the same season.

Voice: Song is a low rattling mechanical trill. Call is *chek* repeated.
Food: Insects. Occasionally small bird eggs.
Nest/Eggs: Ball-shaped nest built with wet reeds, grasses and cattails then lined with plant and feather down, 1-3 feet above ground and secured to aquatic plants. 3-8 eggs.

Nesting Location

Golden-crowned Kinglet

Regulus satrapa

Egg: Actual Size

Backyard Feeder

Birdhouse Nester

Nesting Location

Observation Calendar

J F M A M J J A S O N D

Male: One of the smallest woodland birds, with black head stripes that set off its crown patch of orange with yellow edges; neck and back olive-grey; wings and tail black with olive along edges; feet and legs black; pale grey wingbars; pale eyebrow.
Female: Similar to male except patch on top is yellow.

Did you know? Their movements on a tree make them easy to spot. They flutter their wings as they look for insects.

Voice: Very high-pitched, dropping to a quick chatter. The song is so highly pitched that some people cannot hear it.
Food: A variety of insects, spiders, fruits and seeds.
Nest/Eggs: Deep cup built with moss and lichen at top, lined with black rootlets and feathers suspended from conifer branch, up to 30 metres above ground. 5-11 eggs.

Ruby-crowned Kinglet

Regulus calendula

Observation Calendar

J F M A M J J A S O N D

Male: Olive-grey overall with white eye ring broken at top; crested with red patch on head; chin and neck are lighter olive-grey; feet and legs black; wings and tail black with white edges; white bands on wings.
Female: Similar to male except for no red patch on top of head.

Did you know? The ruby red top on the male is hard to see except when he is courting when, it will flare up.

Voice: High pitched *tee tee tee* followed by a lower *tew tew tew* and ending with a chatter.
Food: Insects, insect eggs, spiders, fruits, seeds.
Nest/Eggs: Deep woven cup built with moss, lichen at top and lined with small black roots and feathers, suspended from conifer branch. 5-10 eggs.

177

Blue-gray Gnatcatcher

Polioptila caerulea

Size Identification

Foot: Anisodactyl

Egg: Actual Size

Observation Calendar
J F M A M J J A S O N D

Male: Overall dark bluish-grey upperparts; white chin, chest and belly; long black tail with white below; white eye ring; sharp black bill; black feet and legs; black eyebrow during mating season.
Female: No black eyebrow during mating season.

Did you know? The Blue-gray Gnatcatcher was named for its feeding behaviour. The bird will dart out from trees and catch gnats and flies in midair.

Voice: Song is a buzzing sound like that a grasshopper makes. Call is *zeeeeee*.
Food: Flying insects, larvae, spiders.
Nest/Eggs: Cup built with spider silk, plant fibres and down then lined with finer materials such as lichen and moss, 0.6-24 metres above ground in fork of tree. 3-6 eggs.

Nesting Location

Eastern Bluebird

Sialia sialis

Size Identification

Foot: Anisodactyl

Egg: Actual Size

Backyard Feeder

Birdhouse Nester

Nesting Location

Observation Calendar

J F M A M J J A S O N D

Male: Bright blue upper parts; tan throat and sides; white belly; feet and legs black.
Female: Similar to male except paler and head has greyish spotting.

Voice: Song is bright whistle *cheer cheerful charmer*. Call is lower *turrweee*.
Food: Variety of insects. Visits feeders for peanut butter, berries, mealworm or raisins.
Nest/Eggs: Built in cavity of tree or birdhouse from a variety of grasses and pine needles, lined with softer material. 3-6 eggs.

Veery

Catharus fuscescens

Foot: Anisodactyl

Egg: Actual Size

Observation Calendar

J F M A M J J A S O N D

Male/Female: Overall reddish-brown upper parts; white buff chest and belly; soft tan spotting along chin and cheeks; grey sides; feet and legs pinkish-grey.

Voice: Soft descending notes — *turreeooreooo-reeoorreeo*. Call is a loud descending *veerr*.
Food: Various insects, larvae, snails, earthworms, spiders and wild berries.
Nest/Eggs: Built of stems, twigs and mosses, lined with softer material including various grasses and rootlets. 3-5 eggs.

Nesting Location

Gray-cheeked Thrush

Catharus minimus

Observation Calendar

J F M A M J J A S O N D

Male/Female: Overall dusty greyish-brown; white neck, chest and belly with bold spotting; faint eye ring; feet and legs pinkish.

Voice: Song is a descending whistle. Call is a descending *weeeoooh*.

Food: Insects, spiders, crayfish, berries, earthworms, caterpillars.

Swainson's Thrush

Catharus ustulatus

Size Identification

Foot: Anisodactyl

Egg: Actual Size

Observation Calendar
J F M A M J J A S O N D

Male/Female: Overall-greyish brown with white belly and throat, which has dark banding; buff eye ring; pink-grey feet and legs.

Did you know? Very vocal bird during feeding. Swainson's Thrush is often seen with large flocks of other birds including warblers.

Voice: Series of rising whistling voice. Short call *whit* and *peeep*.
Food: Insects, fruits, spiders.
Nest/Eggs: Cuplike consisting of grasses, plant fibres and lichens, 1-5 metres above ground. 3-5 eggs.

Nesting Location

Hermit Thrush

Catharus guttatus

Size Identification

Foot: Anisodactyl

Egg: Actual Size

Observation Calendar

J F M A M J J A S O N D

Male/Female: Dusty brown head, neck and back that blends into a rust tail; white eye ring; wings rust when open with black ends; neck and chest white and dark spotted; underparts grey; feet and legs grey with pink; bill black and rust.

Did you know? Not surprisingly, a Hermit Thrush prefers the seclusion of deep wooded areas.

Voice: Sweet song with a variety of phrases. When disturbed it sounds a *kuk kuk kuk kuk*.
Food: A variety of insects, worms, caterpillars, snails and various fruits.
Nest/Eggs: Bulky ground nest built with twigs, bark, grass and moss and lined with conifer needles, fibre and small roots, in damp and cool wooded areas. 3-4 eggs.

Nesting Location

183

Wood Thrush

Hylocichla mustelina

Size Identification

Foot: Anisodactyl

Egg: Actual Size

Observation Calendar

J F M A M J J A S O N D

Male/Female: Rust coloured head fades to a brown back; wings and tail dark brown with black ends; feet and legs grey with pink; black bill has light yellow on underside; white eye ring; chin and chest white with black spotting; underparts grey.

Voice: Suggestive of flute, the song is a series of varied phrases *ee oh lee ee oh lay*.
Food: A variety of insects on the ground and in trees.
Nest/Eggs: Firm and compact cup built with grass, paper, moss, bark and mud, lined with small roots in tree or shrub, 2-15 metres above ground. 3-4 eggs.

Nesting Location

American Robin

Turdus migratorius

Size Identification

Foot: Anisodactyl

Egg: Actual Size

Backyard Feeder

Nesting Location

Observation Calendar

J F M A M J J A S O N D

Male: Charcoal/brown head with distinctive white above and below eye; back and wings charcoal brown with white edges; tail dark grey; neck dark grey with thin white banding; chest and belly brick red; feet and legs black; bill yellow with black at either end.

Female: Breast is slightly paler than male's.

Voice: Song is *cheerily cheerily cheerily* in a whistle tone.

Food: Earthworms, insects, fruit.

Nest/Eggs: Deep cup built with weed stalks, cloth, string and mud, lined with grass, in evergreens and deciduous trees or shrubs. 4 eggs.

Gray Catbird
Dumetella carolinensis

Observation Calendar
J F M A M J J A S O N D

Male/Female: Distinctive black cap with overall grey body; brick red rump which is hidden most of the time; feet and legs grey with hints of pink.

Did you know? Catbirds actually migrate during the night hours and research indicates they use the moon for navigating.

Voice: A distinctive catlike song: *meeow* and *kwut*.
Food: A variety of insects, spiders and wild berries.
Nest/Eggs: Bulky deep cup built with twigs, vines, grass, paper and weeds, lined with small roots, in dense thickets of tree or shrub, 1-3 metres above ground. 3-6 eggs.

Northern Mockingbird

Mimus polyglottos

Observation Calendar

J F M A M J J A S O N D

Male/Female: Grey overall upperparts; white chin, chest and belly; tail long with white edging; reddish-brown eye; feet and legs black. *In flight*: Small white patch on inner part of primaries.

Did you know? The mocking bird gets its name from its habit of mimicking other bird songs, usually repeating them several times.

Voice: Song mimics other song birds. Call is loud *chewk*.
Food: Insects, spiders, snakes and various other reptiles, fruits, berries.
Nest/Eggs: Built of twigs, grasses, dry leaves and various found objects such as cloth, well concealed within a shrub. 2-6 eggs.

187

Brown Thrasher

Size Identification

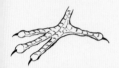
Foot: Anisodactyl

Egg: Actual Size

Observation Calendar
J F M A M J J A S O N D

Male/Female: Distinctive long black bill; grey chin; white chest and belly streaked with dark brown; long reddish-brown tail and back; reddish-brown crown on head; feet and legs pinkish-grey; white and black banding on wings.

Voice: Call is a loud . Voice mimics other birds and is usually repeated twice.
Food: Variety of insects, frogs, lizards, snakes and various wild berries.
Nest/Eggs: Built of twigs, sticks and dead leaves, lined with softer material including grasses and rootlets. 2-6 eggs.

Nesting Location

European Starling

Sturnus vulgaris

Size Identification

Foot: Anisodactyl

Egg: Actual Size

Backyard Feeder

Birdhouse Nester

Nesting Location

Observation Calendar

J F M A M J J A S O N D

Male/Female: *Summer*: Black iridescent bird in summer with light white speckles over entire body; bill is sharp yellow; wing and tail are edged in white and brown; feet and legs are red. *Winter*: Speckles increase and some become brown; bill is black; feet and legs are red; wings and tail have more brown.

Did you know? Sixty starlings were introduced into New York City in 1890. Since then they have spread throughout North America.

Voice: Mimics the songs of other birds and even the sounds of cats and whistles.
Food: A variety of insects, worms, grubs and weed seeds.
Nest/Eggs: Loose cup in cavity filled with grass, leaves, cloth and feathers, up to 18 metres above the ground. 4-5 eggs.

189

American Pipit

Anthus rubescens

Size Identification

Foot: Anisodactyl

Observation Calendar
J F M A M J J A S O N D

Male/Female: *Summer*: Grey-brown on upperparts; light buff breast and belly; chest streaked with brown; buff eyebrow; dark cheek; feet and legs dark brown or black; short brown tail bobs while feeding. *Winter*: Similar to summer except brown upperparts; breast heavily streaked with dark brown.

Voice: Song is repeated *chiweee*. Call is short *peet peet*.
Food: Insects, seeds, weeds, crustaceans, molluscs.

Nesting Location

190

Cedar Waxwing

Bombycilla cedrorum

Size Identification

Foot: Anisodactyl

Egg: Actual Size

Observation Calendar

J F M A M J J A S O N D

Male/Female: Crested brown head with black mask running from black bill, through eyes, to behind head; white outline around mask; back brown; chest and belly yellow-brown; wings black-grey with white edges; wings and tail have red tips; rump white.

Did you know? The name derives from the fact that the wings and tail look as though they have been dipped in red wax.

Voice: Extremely high-pitched *seeee*.
Food: A variety of berries.
Nest/Eggs: Loose woven cup of grass, twigs, cotton fibre and string, lined with small roots, fine grass and down, in open wooded areas in tree or shrub, 2-6 metres above ground. 4-5 eggs.

Nesting Location

191

Blue-winged Warbler

Vermivora pinus

Observation Calendar

J F M A M J J A S O N D

Male/Female: Yellow overall; grey wings; sharp black bill; black line through eye; tail light grey; white undertail coverts; grey feet and legs.

Voice: *Beeee buzzzz* sounding note.
Food: Insects, spiders.
Nest/Eggs: Cone-shaped nest built with grasses, bark and leaves, on or near ground. 5 eggs.

Golden-winged Warbler

Vermivora chrysoptera

Observation Calendar

J F M A M J J A S O N D

Male/Female: Grey overall with bright yellow wing patch; yellow cap; black mask on face with white banding on top and bottom reaching to cheek; feet and legs black.

Voice: Song is buzzing *zeee beee beee*. Call is single *chip*.
Food: Insects, spiders.
Nest/Eggs: Cup-shaped nest built of grasses, leaves and grapevine, hidden on ground. 3-6 eggs.

193

Tennessee Warbler
Vermivora peregrina

Observation Calendar

J F M A M J J A S O N D

Male: Grey upperparts with greenish back; white eyebrow; slightly curved black bill; black feet and legs; green rump with white underparts.
Female: Similar but olive-green overall.

Voice: Loud repeated notes *tsit tsit tsit tsut tsut, tee tee tee*. Call is *chirp*.
Food: Fruit, insects, spiders.

Orange-crowned Warbler

Vermivora celata

Foot: Anisodactyl

Observation Calendar

J F M A M J J A S O N D

Male/Female: Dull olive-green overall; pale olive-yellow underside; faint yellow streaks on side of chest; dark grey feet and legs; orange crown not visible.

Voice: Song is high-pitched trill. Call is *chet*.
Food: Insects, berries.

Nesting Location

Nashville Warbler

Vermivora ruficapilla

Size Identification

Foot: Anisodactyl

Egg: Actual Size

Observation Calendar

J F M A M J J A S O N D

Male/Female: Thin, very pointed bill; head and neck bluish-grey; eye ring white; upper parts olive-green; underparts yellow, white on belly.

Voice: Calls include *see it see it see it*, and *ti ti ti ti ti*.
Food: A variety of insects.
Nest/Eggs: Nest of moss or bark, lined with grass and hair, on ground. 4-5 eggs.

Nesting Location

Yellow Warbler

Dendroica petechia

Size Identification

Foot: Anisodactyl

Egg: Actual Size

Observation Calendar

J F M A M J J A S O N D

Male: Yellow throat and chest; olive back; wings and tail black and olive with yellow highlights; chest barred with chestnut strips; bill and feet reddish-black.
Female: Similar to male only darker and lacks chestnut markings on front chest.

Voice: A sweet and rapid *tsee, tsee, tsee, tsee, titi-wee.*
Food: Insects with large quantities of caterpillars, beetles and moths. Young birds are fed earthworms as well.
Nest/Eggs: Cup of milkweed, hair, down and fine grasses, built in upright fork of tree or bush. 3-6 eggs.

Nesting Location

Chestnut-sided Warbler

Dendroica pensylvanica

Observation Calendar

J F M A M J J A S O N D

Male: Bright lemon-yellow crown with chestnut down sides of chest; black band running through eye from black bill; black and white banding on back with yellow tinting; wings and tail black with white edges; feet and legs black; chin and belly white.
Female: Similar to male except mask is duller and chestnut on sides is reduced.

Did you know? Audubon declared these birds as rare but, with the clearing of woodland, sightings have increased.

Voice: A territorial song—*sweet sweet sweet I so sweet.*
Food: A variety of insects including caterpillars, moths and beetles.
Nest/Eggs: Loose cup of stems, grass and plant down, lined with grass and hair, in briar tangles, hedges or shrubs, up to 2 metres above ground. 3-5 eggs.

Magnolia Warbler

Dendroica magnolia

Size Identification

Foot: Anisodactyl

Egg: Actual Size

Observation Calendar

J F M A M J J A S O N D

Male: Grey head with small eyebrow stripe of white above eye; black mask; yellow chin; chest and belly yellow with black banding; back grey with black banding; wings and tail grey with white edges; two white wing bars; white rump.
Female: Similar to male except banding on chest is narrower; face is grey without black mask and white eyebrow; white eye ring.

Voice: A short melodic song *weeta weeta weeta wee*.
Food: A variety of insects and spiders.
Nest/Eggs: Loosely built cup nest of grass, moss and weed stalks, lined with dark roots, in small conifers along the edge of wooded areas and in gardens. 3-5 eggs.

Nesting Location

Cape May Warbler

Dendroica tigrina

Observation Calendar

J F M A M J J A S O N D

Male: *Spring*: Mostly yellow head with chestnut-orange patch below eye; darker cap; brown and black wings; yellow underparts streaked black; white wing patch; short brown tail. *Fall*: Duller overall but white wing patches still present.
Female: *Spring*: Yellow patch under grey cheek; two narrow white wing bars; paler yellow underparts lightly streaked. *Fall*: Overall dull.

Did you know? The Cape May Warbler will hover at the tips of branches in search of insects.

Voice: High-pitched *seet seeet seeet seet*. Call is high note, *tseee*.
Food: Spruce budworm and other insects.

Black-throated Blue Warbler

Dendroica caerulescens

Size Identification

Foot: Anisodactyl

Egg: Actual Size

Observation Calendar

J F M A M J J A S O N D

Male: Blue-grey head and back; black face mask with black bill; chest white; wings and tail black with white edges; feet and legs black.
Female: Olive-brown head, back and wings with lighter tone on chin, chest and belly; black bill; thin buff eyebrows; feet and legs black; wings and tail olive-brown with white edges.

Voice: A husky song, "I am soo lazzzzy," and a call that is flat *tip*.
Food: A variety of insects, fruits and seeds taken mainly on ground or low-lying branches.
Nest/Eggs: Bulky cup of spider's web, dead wood, twigs, leaves and grass, lined with dark rootlets, in tree or shrub close to ground. 3-5 eggs.

Nesting Location

Foot: Anisodactyl

Egg: Actual Size

Yellow-rumped Warbler

Dendroica coronata

Observation Calendar

J F M A M J J A S O N D

Male/Female: *Spring*: Yellow rump and yellow patch on either side of chest; yellow crest set against grey head; black mask running from black bill; back grey with black banding; wings and tail black with white edges; two white wing bars; chin white; chest white with black band; feet and legs charcoal; white eyebrow. *Fall*: Similar but duller markers, no black mask, more brown and buff overall.

Did you know? This very abundant warbler was once called Myrtle Warbler and was thought to be two different species because of its change of plumage.

Voice: Song is light musical notes. Call is *cheeeck*.
Food: A variety of insects and fruit.
Nest/Eggs: Deep cup of twigs, bark, plant down and fibres, lined with hair, feathers and fine grass, in tree or shrub near trunk. 3-5 eggs.

Nesting Location

Black-throated Green Warbler

Dendroica virens

Observation Calendar

J F M A M J J A S O N D

Male: Olive head and back; yellow around eyes and on cheeks; black throat and chest changing to speckled black on white on belly and chest; black banding along sides of belly; wings and tail are black with white edging; two white wing bars; feet and legs brown-black; white rump.

Female: Yellow on throat with minimal black.

Voice: Song has a variety of accents, *zee zee zee zuu zee*, and sounds like "sleep sleep little one sleep."

Food: Variety of insects and fruit.

Nest/Eggs: Compact cup of fine bark, twigs, grass, lichens and spider's web, lined with hair, fur, feathers and small roots, in tree or shrub, 1-25 metres above ground. 3-5 eggs.

Blackburnian Warbler

Dendroica fusca

Observation Calendar

J F M A M J J A S O N D

Male: Bright orange-yellow chin, top of head and eyebrow set against black; black band running through eye; back black with white banding; wings and tail black with white edges; large white band on wing; feet and legs red and black; rump white.
Female: Similar to male except orange-yellow is paler; cheeks grey; belly grey.

Voice: Variable song is high-pitched and thin with a mixture of signal chirps and trills, *tsip tsip tsip titi tzeeeeee.*
Food: A variety of insects and berries.
Nest/Eggs: Cup nest built with plant down and spider's web, lined with hair, small roots and grass, in tree or shrub, 25 metres above ground. 4-5 eggs.

Pine Warbler

Dendroica pinus

Size Identification

Foot: Anisodactyl

Egg: Actual Size

Backyard Feeder

Nesting Location

Observation Calendar

J F M A M J J A S O N D

Male/Female: Olive-green upperparts; yellow chin, chest and belly; dark wings with two rows of white wing bands; feet and legs black.

Did you know? The Pine Warbler's name is derived from the fact that it is usually seen in pine trees and is fairly common in mature pine plantations.

Voice: Song is a trill in same key.
Food: Insects, spiders, fruit, berries.
Nest/Eggs: Cup-shaped nest built of twigs, bark, grasses and pine needles in a pine tree. 3-5 eggs.

Palm Warbler

Dendroica palmarum

Size Identification

Foot: Anisodactyl

Observation Calendar
J F M A M J J A S O N D

Male/Female: *Spring:* Rust crown that changes to brown on back of head and back; bright yellow eyebrow; brown cheeks; yellow chin and chest with rust speckles; yellow belly; rump yellow; wings and tail black and brown with white edges; feet and legs black; black bill. *Fall:* Overall browner and duller.

Did you know? The Palm Warbler is nicknamed the "wagtail warbler" and "yellow tip-up" because of its habit of bobbing its tail continuously while feeding.

Voice: Song is *zee zee zee* that rises. Call is sharp *suuup*.
Food: A variety of insects and weed seeds.
Nest/Eggs: Nest of dry grass and weed stalks, lined with fine grass, at the base of a tree or shrub. 3-5 eggs.

Nesting Location

Bay-breasted Warbler

Dendroica castanea

Observation Calendar

J F M A M J J A S O N D

Male: *Spring:* Deep rust patch on top of black head; rust on chin and along sides of chest; grey back with black banding; two white wing bars; wings and tail are black with white edges; belly white with soft rust on sides; rump white; buff patch on either side of neck; feet and legs black with hints of red. *Fall:* head changes to olive/yellow; back is yellow/olive; chest is white with pink on sides; rump is buff.
Female: Duller with less rust on neck and sides.

Did you know? The quickest way to identify the Bay-breasted Warbler is to locate the buff patch on the side of the neck.

Voice: Difficult to distinguish from other warblers. Song is high pitched *seetsy seetsy seetsy*. Call *see*.
Food: A variety of tree-dwelling insects.
Nest/Eggs: Loosely woven cup nest built of twigs, dried grass and spider's web, lined with small roots, hair and fine grasses, in tree or shrub, 4-8 metres above ground. 4-7 eggs.

Blackpoll Warbler

Dendroica striata

Observation Calendar

J F M A M J J A S O N D

Male: *Spring*: Black head with white cheeks; back grey with black banding; wings and tail black with white edges; chin white; chest white with black banding; rump white; two white wing bars; feet and legs black and red. *Fall*: Olive-green overall with light banding on sides.

Female: Olive on top with thin black banding; back olive with black banding; wings and tail black with white edges, two white wing bands; chin and chest grey with small specks of black; belly grey.

Voice: High-pitched *zi zi zi zi zi* growing louder. Call is *chip.*
Food: A variety of insects.
Nest/Eggs: Bulky cup built with small twigs, grasses, weeds and moss, lined with hair, plant fibres and feathers, in conifer tree or shrub, about 2 metres above ground. 4-5 eggs.

Cerulean Warbler

Dendroica cerulea

Size Identification

Foot: Anisodactyl

Egg: Actual Size

Observation Calendar

J F M A M J J A S O N D

Male: Cerulean (sky-blue) upperparts; black streaks along white chest; black breast band; white wing bars; grey feet and legs.
Female: Turquoise-blue upperparts; bluish crown; light cream chest and belly with faded banding.

Voice: Medium-pitched quick *buzzzzz* sound ending with high note. Call is *chip*.
Food: Flying insects.
Nest/Eggs: Saucer built with grasses, tree bark and weeds high in the canopy of deciduous trees. 3-5 eggs.

Nesting Location

Black-and-white Warbler

Mniotilta varia

Size Identification

Foot: Anisodactyl

Egg: Actual Size

Observation Calendar

J F M A M J J A S O N D

Male: Black-and-white striped from crown down entire body length; feet and legs charcoal; bill is thin and black with thin yellow line at mouth opening.

Female: Similar to the male except striping on chest and belly is grey and white, throat is white.

Voice: Seven or more squeaky calls *weesee, weesee, weesee, weesee, weesee, weesee, weesee.*

Food: A variety of insects, mainly gypsy moths and tent caterpillars.

Nest/Eggs: Cup built of leaves, grass, hair and bark, at base of tree or near a boulder. 4-5 eggs.

Nesting Location

American Redstart

Setophaga ruticilla

Observation Calendar

J F M A M J J A S O N D

Male: Black overall with large orange bands on wings and outer tail feathers; bright red/orange patch on side of chest; belly white; feet and legs black.
Female: Overall olive-grey with large yellow bands on wings and tail; white eyering, broken; yellow on sides of white chest; white belly; feet and legs black.

Voice: Song is a series of high-pitched thin notes ending downward. Call is *chip*.
Food: A variety of insects, wild berries and seeds.
Nest/Eggs: Compact woven cup built with plant down and grass, lined with weeds, hair and feathers, covered on the outside with lichens, plant down and spider's web, in woodlands and swamps. 4 eggs.

211

Prothonotary Warbler

Protonotaria citrea

Size Identification

Foot: Anisodactyl

Egg: Actual Size

Birdhouse Nester

Nesting Location

Observation Calendar

J F M A M J J A S O N D

Male: Bright yellow overall; black-grey wings and tail; sharp black bill; feet and legs black; white highlights in tail and underparts.
Female: Similar but with olive highlights on crown, nape and back; grey wings.

Did you know? The Prothonotary Warbler prefers to build its nest in an abandoned woodpecker hole.

Voice: Loud *zweeet*, repeated in a series at the same pitch. Call is a loud *tinc*.
Food: Insects, spiders.
Nest/Eggs: Cavity built and lined with twigs, mosses and grasses. 4-6 eggs.

Ovenbird

Seiurus aurocapillas

Observation Calendar

J F M A M J J A S O N D

Male/Female: Olive overall with distinctive mark on head that is orange outlined in black, running from bill to the back of the neck; chest white with black speckles; bill dark on top with yellow on underside; black eyes surrounded by white.

Voice: A progressively louder, *teecher, teecher, teecher, teecher.*
Food: Snails, slugs, worms, spiders and most insects.
Nest/Eggs: Covered bowl, with side entry made of dead leaves, grass, moss and bark, lined with small roots, fibres and hair, on ground in depression. 3-5 eggs.

Northern Waterthrush

Seiurus noveboracensis

Observation Calendar

J F M A M J J A S O N D

Male/Female: Brown head and back with distinctive yellow eyebrow running to back of head; chest pale yellow with dark pronounced banding running down to lower belly; legs pink and red; bill black and pink; short tail.

Voice: A ringing song which drops off at the end. Call is a metallic *chink.*
Food: A variety of insects and water bugs, crustaceans, small fish, mollusks.
Nest/Eggs: Cup or dome of moss, twigs, bark and leaves, lined with moss, hair and fine grass, on ground in upturned roots or fallen trees. 4-5 eggs.

Mourning Warbler

Oporornis philadelphia

Size Identification

Foot: Anisodactyl

Egg: Actual Size

Observation Calendar

J F M A M J J A S O N D

Male: Grey hood with olive back; yellow chest and belly with black collar; bill black with pale underparts; wings and tail dark with yellow edges; feet and legs brown.
Female: Hood is duller; broken white eye ring; wings and tail olive ending in black with white edges; chest pale grey.

Voice: Loud ringing *chirry chirry chirry chorry.*
Food: A variety of insects and spiders.
Nest/Eggs: Bulky cup of leaves, vines, grass, weeds and bark, lined with fine grasses, rootlets and hair, on or near ground. 3-5 eggs.

Nesting Location

Common Yellowthroat
Geothlypis trichas

Foot: Anisodactyl

Egg: Actual Size

Male: Yellow chin, chest and belly contrast with a dark black mask, which runs from bill, around eyes to lower neck; white line blends into an olive head, back, wings and tail; feet and legs grey.
Female: Light brown without the distinctive mask.

Voice: A very high-pitched song, *witchity witchity witchity* that is heavily accented.
Food: Caterpillars, beetles, ants and other small insects.
Nest/Eggs: Bulky cup of grass, reeds, leaves and moss, lined with grass and hair, on or near ground, in weed stalks or low bushes. 3-5 eggs.

Nesting Location

Hooded Warbler

Wilsonia citrina

Observation Calendar

J F M A M J J A S O N D

Male/Female: Distinct yellow mask set against black head; large black eye; chest and belly yellow; greenish-olive back; feet and legs black.

Voice: Two note *wee-taa* repeated. Call is *chink*.
Food: Flying insects on the wing, other insects, spiders.
Nest/Eggs: Cup-shaped nest built of dried leaves, twigs and plant fibres, in a shrub. 3-5 eggs.

Wilson's Warbler

Wilsonia pusilla

Observation Calendar
J F M A M J J A S O N D

Male: Black patch on top of olive-green head; back olive-green; face, cheeks, chin and belly yellow; wings and tail black with white and yellow edges; feet and legs red-pink; short bill, black with red along opening.
Female: Similar to male except the amount of black patch on top varies.

Voice: Song is a short series of *chet chet chet*.
Food: A variety of insects, including flying insects, and berries.
Nest/Eggs: Concealed cup nest built of grass, leaves and some hair, on ground at base of tree. 4-6 eggs.

Canada Warbler

Wilsonia canadensis

Observation Calendar
J F M A M J J A S O N D

Male: Dark greyish-blue head and back; eyes have white and yellow ring; black under eyes; yellow under chin extends to lower belly with a band of black speckles across chest similar to a necklace; wings and tail black edged in white; black bill has grey underside; white rump.

Female: Duller overall with black speckled necklace across chest being very faint.

Voice: Richly varied musical song starting with a chip.

Food: A variety of insects including beetles, mosquitoes and larvae of moths and flies.

Nest/Eggs: Bulky cup nest built of weeds, bark and leaves, lined with rootlets, plant down and hair, on or near ground in moss-covered area. 3-5 eggs.

Yellow-breasted Chat

Icteria virens

Size Identification

Foot: Anisodactyl

Egg: Actual Size

Observation Calendar

Male/Female: Olive-green upperparts; yellow chin and breast; white belly and rump; white eyebrow; black feet and legs.

Food: Insects, fruits, berries.
Voice: Various whistles and rattling sounds. Call is *chack*.
Nest/Eggs: Bulky cup of leaves built with shredded straw and grasses in small tree or bush. 3-5 eggs.

Nesting Location

Scarlet Tanager
Piranga olivacea

Size Identification

Foot: Anisodactyl

Egg: Actual Size

Observation Calendar

J F M A M J J A S O N D

Male: Scarlet red from head to rump with dark black wings and tail; bill is dull yellow; feet and legs black.
Female: Olive-yellow overall with black-grey wings and tail.

Voice: Call is a *chip burr* while its song is a buzzing *querit queer queery querit queer* that is well spaced out.
Food: A variety of insects and fruit.
Nest/Eggs: Flat and flimsy cup nest on farthest branches in tree or shrub, sometimes far from the ground. 3-5 eggs.

Nesting Location

221

Eastern Towhee
Pipilo erythrophthalmus

Size Identification

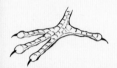

Foot: Anisodactyl

Egg: Actual Size

Backyard Feeder

Birdhouse Nester

Nesting Location

Observation Calendar
J F M A M J J A S O N D

Male: Distinctive black head with black bill; rust-red sides and vent; white belly; feet and legs pinkish-grey; black back with white banding; long black tail with white oval-shaped underparts.

Female: Similar to male but with brown head, back and tail; white belly.

Voice: Whistle followed by a trill in two notes. Sounds like "drink your tea." Call is a quick chewink.

Food: Variety of insects, snakes, lizards, weeds and spiders.

Nest/Eggs: Built of twigs and leaves with softer grasses lining inside, placed in depression in ground. 2-6 eggs.

American Tree Sparrow

Spizella arborea

Size Identification

Foot: Anisodactyl

Observation Calendar

J F M A M J J A S O N D

Male/Female: Rust on top of head with light grey face, rust band running through eye; chin, chest and belly grey with a faint dark grey spot on chest; wings and tail brown and black with white edge; two white wing bars; short pointed bill is grey on top with yellow underside; feet and legs are red-black, rump grey.

Voice: Call is te el wit.
Food: A variety of weed seeds and tree seeds.
Nest/Eggs: Cup nest, low in tree or shrub. 4 eggs.

Backyard Feeder

Nesting Location

223

Chipping Sparrow
Spizella passerina

Size Identification

Foot: Anisodactyl

Egg: Actual Size

Backyard Feeder

Observation Calendar
J F M A M J J A S O N D

Male/Female: Summer: Bright rust crown with grey face that has a black band running through eye; short pointed bill is black; chin white changing to grey for chest and belly; feet and legs pink with black; white eyebrow; wings and tail black with brown and white edges; back brown banding with black. Winter: Rust crown becomes duller turning brown with black streaks; bill is pale yellow and black; eyebrow changes to buff; underside changes to buff.

Voice: Song is short trill.
Food: A variety of insects on the ground. Occasionally snatches flying insects.
Nest/Eggs: Cup built with grass, weed stalks and small roots, lined with hair and grass, low in tree or shrub, up to 8 metres above ground. 4 eggs.

Nesting Location

Field Sparrow

Spizella pusilla

Foot: Anisodactyl

Egg: Actual Size

Observation Calendar

J F M A M J J A S O N D

Male/Female: Overall brown with grey speckles; reddish-brown cap; distinctive white eye ring; bright pink bill; feet and legs pinkish-grey; tail dark with brown highlights; white vent and lower belly.

Voice: Whistles descending and gradually increasing in speed. Calls are chip and trills.
Food: Various insects and seeds. May visit feeders if seeds have fallen to ground.
Nest/Eggs: Cuplike, built from a variety of grasses and positioned on ground. 3-4 eggs.

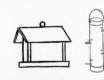

Backyard Feeder

Birdhouse Nester

Nesting Location

225

Vesper Sparrow

Pooecetes gramineus

Size Identification

Foot: Anisodactyl

Egg: Actual Size

Observation Calendar
J F M A M J J A S O N D

Male/Female: Light grey overall with very fine streaks of black running down entire body; short pointed bill black on top with grey underside; feet and legs grey; back banded with black; wings and tail dark grey with white edges; white ring and small chestnut patch near shoulder; white tail feathers are revealed in flight.

Did you know? The Vesper Sparrow earned its name from its song that may be heard in the evening — at vespers, when evening prayers were said in the monasteries.

Voice: A whistle of two beats, with the second being higher, followed by trills.
Food: A variety of insects, weed seeds and grain.
Nest/Eggs: Depression in ground with grass, stalks and small roots, and lined with the same. 4 eggs.

Savannah Sparrow

Passerculus sandwichensis

Observation Calendar

J F M A M J J A S O N D

Male/Female: Black, brown and white central stripe on head; back brown with black banding; chin, chest and belly streaked with black and brown; wings and tail black with brown edges; tail is notched; bright yellow eyebrow; feet and legs red; short pointed bill is black and pink; white eye ring.

Voice: A faint, lisping tsit tsit tsit tseeeee tsaaaay.

Food: Main diet consists of weed seeds but will eat a variety of insects, spiders and snails.

Nest/Eggs: Scratched hollow in ground filled with grass, lined with finer grass, hair and small roots. 3-6 eggs.

Grasshopper Sparrow

Ammodramus savannarum

Size Identification

Foot: Anisodactyl

Egg: Actual Size

Backyard Feeder

Nesting Location

Observation Calendar
J F M A M J J A S O N D

Male/Female: Overall brown mottled; white underparts with buff sides; chin white; dark crown with buff streaking; feet and legs pink, short tail.

Did you know? The Grasshopper Sparrow got its name from the buzzing sound it makes during courtship.

Voice: High pitched buzzzzz.
Food: Seeds, insects.
Nest/Eggs: Cup-shaped nest built with grass and rootlets, then lined with finer materials including grass and hair, in shallow depression on ground. 4-5 eggs.

Song Sparrow

Melospiza melodia

Size Identification

Foot: Anisodactyl

Egg: Actual Size

Backyard Feeder

Nesting Location

Observation Calendar

J F M A M J J A S O N D

Male/Female: Brown head and back streaked with black; buff-grey eyebrow extending to back of neck; brown band running through eye; chin, chest and belly are white with brown-black banding running down to lower belly; short pointed bill is black on top with yellow underside; red-brown crown with central white stripe; wings and tail brown with white edges; feet and legs pink; long rounded tail.

Did you know? Thoreau 'interpreted' this sparrow's song as "Maids! Maids! Maids! hang up your teakettle-ettle-ettle."

Voice: Call is a variety which includes tsip and tchump. Song is a variety of rich notes.
Food: A variety of insects, weed seeds and fruit.
Nest/Eggs: Cup close to ground with weeds, leaves and bark, lined with grass roots and hair, in tree or shrub, less than 4 metres from ground. 3-5 eggs.

Lincoln's Sparrow

Melospiza lincolnii

Size Identification

Foot: Anisodactyl

Observation Calendar

J F M A M J J A S O N D

Male/Female: Rust on top of head with thin grey central streak; dark grey face; buff across chest and down sides of belly with fine black streaking; belly white; feet and legs pink; wing and tail feathers black with brown edges.

Voice: Wild mixture of trills and buzzing. Calls include tsup and zeee.

Food: A variety of weed seeds and insects.

Nest/Eggs: Flat ground in bundle of grass. Built with grass, moss and lichen, lined with fine grass. 3-6 eggs.

Backyard Feeder

Nesting Location

Swamp Sparrow

Melospiza georgiana

Foot: Anisodactyl

Egg: Actual Size

Observation Calendar

J F M A M J J A S O N D

Male/Female: Summer: Top of head is reddish-brown and black; face grey with black streaks; black bill is small and sharp; chin and chest white-grey with rust along sides; back brown with black banding; wings and tail feathers brown with black ends and white edges; feet and legs pink; grey eyebrows. Winter: Similar to summer but both sides of chest turn darker brown and top of head is streaked with black and brown, with grey central stripe.

Put on your hip waders to spot this bird. It spends its summers near swamps and bogs.

Voice: Song is an unbroken musical trill. Call is chip.
Food: A variety of insects and seeds.
Nest/Eggs: Bulky cup built with grass, lined with finer grass, in tussock of grass or in low shrub. 3-6 eggs.

Nesting Location

White-throated Sparrow

Zonotrichia albicollis

Size Identification

Foot: Anisodactyl

Egg: Actual Size

Backyard Feeder

Observation Calendar

J F M A M J J A S O N D

Male/Female: Top of head is black with white central stripe; white eyebrows on either side that begin with yellow tint; black band running through eye followed by grey cheeks; small white bib under chin; grey chest; white belly with faint banding; wings and tail feathers black and brown with white edges; feet pink; back brown banded with black.

Voice: Whistle is teeet teeet tetodi tetodi teetodi. Calls are tseet.

Food: A variety of insects, grain, weed seeds and fruit.

Nest/Eggs: Cup built of grass, small roots, pine needles, twigs, bark and moss, lined with small roots, hair and grass. 3-5 eggs.

Nesting Location

White-crowned Sparrow

Zonotrichia leucophrys

Observation Calendar

J F **M A M J J A S O** N D

Male/Female: Black and white streaked head; brown and black mottled back; light grey chin, chest and belly; feet and legs yellow.

Did you know? For a week or two in May the White-crowned Sparrow is a fairly common visitor to backyards.

Voice: Whistled notes and call that includes a sharp-sounding pink.
Food: Seeds, insects.

Dark-eyed Junco

Junco hyemalis

Egg: Actual Size

Backyard Feeder

Observation Calendar
J F M A M J J A S O N D

Male: Dark charcoal overall with white belly; short sharp bill is pale yellow with black at end; feet and legs dark grey; tail has white outer feathers that can be seen in flight.
Female: May be slightly paler than male.

Voice: Song is a trill in short phrases. Calls are tsip, zeeet or keew keew.
Food: A variety of insects, weed seeds and wild fruit.
Nest/Eggs: Large and compact built with grass, rootlets and hair, lined with hair, concealed low to or on ground. 4-5 eggs.

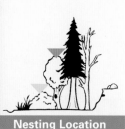

Nesting Location

Snow Bunting
Plectrophenax nivalis

Size Identification

Foot: Anisodactyl

Observation Calendar
J F M A M J J A S O N D

Male: Summer: White overall with black wings and tail; tail has white edges; wings have large white patches on shoulder and flight feathers; feet and legs black; black bill, short and sharp. In flight: wings white.
Female and male in winter have brown and rust blotches.

Did you know? Accustomed to cold and heavy snowfall, the Snow Bunting will dig a hole in the snow to escape from a storm.

Voice: Song is a chorus of whistles. Call includes buzzy tew.
Food: A variety of insects, tree buds and seeds.
Nest/Eggs: Cup, low to ground, in tree or shrub. 3-5 eggs.

Nesting Location

Northern Cardinal

Cardinalis cardinalis

Size Identification

Foot: Anisodactyl

Egg: Actual Size

Backyard Feeder

Nesting Location

Observation Calendar

J F M A M J J A S O N D

Male: Brilliant red overall with a stout red-orange bill, crested head; black mask beginning at base of bill resembling a small bib; feet dark red.

Female: Buff and grey with hints of bright red on crest, wings and back; stout red-orange bill with black mask beginning at base of bill (bib may appear smaller); feet are dark red.

Did you know? The cardinal gets its name from its bright red colour, which resembles that of the robes and hat of a Roman Catholic cardinal.

Voice: Song is a series of repeated whistles wheit wheit wheit, cheer cheer cheer. Also chip.

Food: Seeds, fruits, grains, various insects.

Nest/Eggs: Woven cup of twigs, vines, leaves and grass, 2-3 metres above ground, in dense shrubbery. 2-5 eggs.

Rose-breasted Grosbeak

Pheucticus ludovicianus

Size Identification

Foot: Anisodactyl

Egg: Actual Size

Backyard Feeder

Nesting Location

Observation Calendar

J F M A M J J A S O N D

Male: Large, pale yellow bill with black head; red V shape on chest; belly white with rust on either side; wings and tail black with white at edges of tail feathers visible in flight; white patches on wings; rump white; feet and legs charcoal.
Female: Buff eyebrow that extends to back of neck; brown head and back with shade of black; wings and tail brown with white edges; two white wing bars; chest and belly speckled brown; feet and legs charcoal.

Did you know? The Rose-breasted Grosbeak is a fierce competitor when mating, clashing violently with other males. However, when it comes time to sit on the nest, the males have been known to sing.

Voice: Similar to a robin but rapid notes that are continuous cheer-e-ly cheer-e-ly. Call is chink chink.
Food: A variety of insects, tree buds, fruit and wild seeds.
Nest/Eggs: Woven grass cup in fork of deciduous tree or shrub, close to the ground. 3-6 eggs.

Indigo Bunting

Passerina cyanea

Size Identification

Foot: Anisodactyl

Egg: Actual Size

Observation Calendar
J F M A M J J A S O N D

Male: Medium to deep turquoise blue overall; wide, sharp, grey beak; feet and legs black; wings and tail dark with blue highlights.
Female: Soft brown overall; buff sides and belly; faint wing bands; short conical grey beak.

Voice: Rapid series of whistles that are short and paired together — tse tsee tew tew. Call is short spiit.
Food: Insects, seeds, grain, berries.
Nest/Eggs: Compact woven cup built from stems, grasses and leaves, lined with down, in thick vegetation. 2-6 eggs.

Nesting Location

Bobolink

Dolichonyx oryzivorus

Size Identification

Foot: Anisodactyl

Egg: Actual Size

Observation Calendar

J F M A M J J A S O N D

Male: Summer: Black overall with pale yellow patch on back of head; back black changing to large white patch down to rump; wings have white patches and edges; feet, legs, and bill black. In flight: White rump is revealed; tail has sharp pointed feathers. **Female and male** (winter): brown and buff overall with black streaks over top of head; legs red.

Did you know? These birds need hayfield habitat to survive. Studies show that most young will die when farmers' fields are mown before they have a chance to fledge.

Voice: Song is a light phrase that increases in pitch and has been described as bob o link - bob o link spink spank spink. Usually sings in flight. Call is metallic clink.
Food: A variety of insects and weed seeds
Nest/Eggs: Slight hollow in ground with bulky gathering of grass and weed stalks, lined with fine grass, in areas near water and within waterside plants. 4-7 eggs.

Nesting Location

Red-winged Blackbird

Agelaius phoeniceus

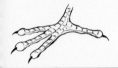

Observation Calendar

J F M A M J J A S O N D

Male: Black overall with distinctive red shoulder patch bordered with light yellow at bottom.
Female: Brown with buff eyebrows and chin; chest and belly buff streaked with dark brown; wings and tail feathers brown with buff edges.

Did you know? Red-winged Blackbirds are prolific breeders, sometimes breeding three times in one season.

Voice: Song is ocaaleee ocaalee.
Food: A variety of insects and weed seeds.
Nest/Eggs: Bulky cup built of leaves, rushes, grass, rootlets, moss and milkweed fibre, lined with grass, in tall waterside plants near water. 3-4 eggs.

Eastern Meadowlark
Sturnella magna

Size Identification

Foot: Anisodactyl

Egg: Actual Size

Backyard Feeder

Birdhouse Nester

Nesting Location

Observation Calendar

J F M A M J J A S O N D

Male/Female: Bright yellow chin and throat separated by a V-shaped black collar; black on top of head with white cheeks; yellow and black band runs through eye; sides white with black speckles; back and wings black and brown with white edges; feet and legs grey; black bill is long and thin with grey underside.

Voice: Song is teee yuuu teee yaar repeated two to eight times.
Food: A variety of insects including grubs, beetles, grasshoppers and caterpillars. Also eats seeds and grain.
Nest/Eggs: Bulky cup in hollow on the ground in pastures, fields and marshes. Dome-shaped with a roof of interwoven grasses. 3-5 eggs.

Rusty Blackbird
Euphagus carolinus

Size Identification

Foot: Anisodactyl

Observation Calendar

J F M A M J J A S O N D

Male: Dull black overall with hints of green on head and bluish on wings; pale yellow eye; pointed black bill; short tail rounded at end; feet and legs black. Winter: Similar to summer but feathers edged in brown along with brown hints on head and wings.

Female: Overall light brown/grey with darker wings; slate-grey underparts; buff eyebrow; feet and legs black.

Did you know? The Rusty Blackbird will form large flocks in winter along with starlings and other blackbirds.

Voice: Song is extremely squeaky koo-a-lee-meek koo-a-lee eek, with call that is chuk or kick.

Food: Insects, salamanders, snails, small fish, grains, seeds, crustaceans.

Nest/Eggs: Small cup built from grasses and moss with a mud lining mixed with fine grass materials. Builds 2-10 feet above ground in bush or small tree usually above water. 4-5 eggs.

Nesting Location

242

Common Grackle

Quiscalus quiscula

Size Identification

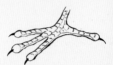

Foot: Anisodactyl

Egg: Actual Size

Backyard Feeder

Nesting Location

Observation Calendar
J F M A M J J A S O N D

Male: Overall iridescent black and purple; bright yellow eye; black bill long and sharp; feet and legs are charcoal grey; long tail.
Female: Similar but duller iridescent colouring, tail is shorter.

Did you know? Flocks in the thousands gather on fields and cause a lot of damage to farmers' crops.

Voice: Chatter is a metallic and rasping grideleeeeek. Calls are chak chah.
Food: A variety of ground insects, seeds, grain, minnows, rodents and crayfish.
Nest/Eggs: Loose bulky cup built with weed stalks, twigs, grass, debris, lined with feather and grass, in conifer tree or shrubs. Will occasionally use an osprey's nest. Prefers to nest in colonies. 3-6 eggs.

Brown-headed Cowbird

Molothrus ater

Size Identification

Foot: Anisodactyl

Egg: Actual Size

Observation Calendar
J F M A M J J A S O N D

Male: Brown head, glossy black overall; feet and legs black; sharp black bill.
Female: Overall grey with dark brown wings and tail; faint buff streaking on chest down to lower belly; feet and legs are black.

Did you know? Molothrus ater, the Cowbird's scientific name, means dark, greedy beggar, an apt name for a bird that leaves its eggs for other birds to hatch.

Voice: A squeaky weee titi.
Food: A variety of insects, weed seeds, grain and grass.
Nest/Eggs: Parasite. Builds no nest. 1 egg.

Nesting Location

244

Baltimore Oriole

Icterus galbula

Size Identification

Foot: Anisodactyl

Egg: Actual Size

Backyard Feeder

Nesting Location

Observation Calendar

J F M A M J J A S O N D

Male: Black head; bright orange body; black wings with orange spur and white banding; tail is black with orange along edges; legs and feet grey; long sharp grey beak.

Female: Browner than male with olive-yellow on rump; orange-yellow chest and belly; head and back mix of black, orange and brown; throat blotched; tail brown-orange.

Did you know? Baltimore Orioles can be attracted to feeders with orange slices or sugar solutions.

Voice: Song is a note whistled four to eight times. Call is a two-note teetoo and rapid chatter ch ch ch ch.

Food: Insects, flower nectar, fruit.

Nest/Eggs: Plant fibre that hangs from branches. 4-6 eggs.

Purple Finch

Carpodacus purpureus

Size Identification

Foot: Anisodactyl

Egg: Actual Size

Backyard Feeder

Observation Calendar
J F M A M J J A S O N D

Male: Red upper parts with black banding on back; rump is red; chest is red with white feathers banding down to lower belly, which is all white; wings and tail are black with white edges; bill is broad and yellow; feet and legs grey.
Female: Brown with white eyebrow and brown eyeline; chest white with brown streaks down front; wings and tail dull brown with white edges; feet and legs grey.

Voice: Song is long and musical ending in downward trill. Call chirp.
Food: A variety of insects, berries, weed seeds, and buds of trees.
Nest/Eggs: Shallow cup built with twigs, grass, bark strips and small roots, lined with grass and hair, in evergreen tree or shrub, 5-60 feet above ground. 3-5 eggs.

Nesting Location

House Finch
Carpodacus mexicanus

Size Identification

Foot: Anisodactyl

Egg: Actual Size

Observation Calendar

J F M A M J J A S O N D

Male: Red crown, chin and chest, which changes to buff at belly; wings and tail brown; feet and legs grey; grey bill; white undertail; dark brown banding around the sides.
Female: All greyish brown with faint banding down sides.

Voice: Musical warble ending with jeeeeer.
Food: Weed seeds, fruit, buds.
Nest/Eggs: Cup of lined weed and grass, roots, feathers, string and twigs, 1-2 metres above ground. 4-5 eggs.

Backyard Feeder

Nesting Location

White-winged Crossbill

Loxia leucoptera

Size Identification

Foot: Anisodactyl

Egg: Actual Size

Backyard Feeder

Observation Calendar
J F M A M J J A S O N D

Male: Overall pinkish-red with long black bill that crosses over at the end; wings and tail black, with two large white bars; lower belly turns grey; feet and legs charcoal.
Female: Similar to male except greyish with olive areas on back and head, yellow on chest and rump.

Did you know? Their bills are used to extract conifer seeds by forcing open the cone and pulling seeds out. It is an occasional breeder in the area and seen erratically.

Appear in large numbers in wooded areas near the shore.

Voice: Call to each other peeet with a flight call of chif chif.
Food: Conifer seeds, variety of insects, other seeds.
Nest/Eggs: Deep cup built with twigs, small roots, weed stalks, moss, lichen, and bark, lined with grass, feather and hair, in spruce tree or shrub, 2-3 metres above ground. 2-5 eggs.

Nesting Location

Common Redpoll

Carduelis flammea

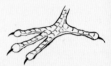

Observation Calendar

J F M A M J J A S O N D

Male: Red to orange cap; brown streaking on white overall; black/brown wings with two narrow wing bars; black chin; bright rose breast and sides; brown banding on sides.
Female: Red to orange cap; brown on back of head; breast is light with brown banding down sides.

Voice: Series of trills includes chit during flight, chit-chit-chit-chit. Call is sweeeeet.
Food: A variety of grass, tree and weed seeds, as well as insects in summer.
Nest/Eggs: Cup shape built of small twigs and lined with softer materials including moss, plant material and animal fur. Built in dense brush low to the ground. 4-7 eggs.

Pine Siskin

Carduelis pinus

Size Identification

Foot: Anisodactyl

Egg: Actual Size

Backyard Feeder

Nesting Location

Observation Calendar
J F M A M J J A S O N D

Male/Female: Brown with buff chest and belly banded with brown; long pointed bill is grey; wings and tail dark with yellow edges; feet and legs grey.

Did you know? Two points of identification of the Pine Siskin are its size and the song, which it sings in flight.

Voice: Light rasping tit i tit and louder cleeeip. Similar to a Goldfinch but deeper and coarser.
Food: Conifer seeds, weed seeds, nectar, flower buds and a variety of insects.
Nest/Eggs: Large shallow cup built with twigs, grass, moss, lichen, bark and small roots, lined with moss, hair and feathers in a conifer tree well out from trunk, 6 metres above ground. 2-6 eggs.

250

American Goldfinch

Carduelis tristis

Size Identification

Foot: Anisodactyl

Egg: Actual Size

Backyard Feeder

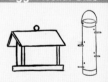

Observation Calendar
J F M A M J J A S O N D

Male: Summer: Bright yellow overall with black forehead and yellow bill; black wings with white bands; tail black with white edges; rump white; feet and legs red. Winter: Yellow is replaced by grey with hints of yellow.
Female and male (winter): Similar except overall grey/brown with yellow highlights.

Voice: Sing as they fly with a succession of chips and twitters, per chic o ree per chic o ree.
Food: A variety of insects but mostly interested in thistle and weed seeds.
Nest/Eggs: Neat cup built with fibres woven together, lined with thistle and feather down, in leafy tree or shrub in upright branches, 1-5 metres above ground. 4-6 eggs.

Nesting Location

Evening Grosbeak
Coccothraustes vespertinus

Size Identification

Foot: Anisodactyl

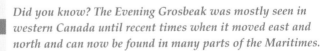

Observation Calendar
J F M A M J J A S O N D

Male: Dark brown/black head with dull yellow stripe across forehead that blends into a dull yellow at the shoulders; tail and wings are black with hints of white; chest and stomach dull yellow; stout pale yellow bill and dark pink feet.
Female: Silver grey with light hints of dull yellow on neck and sides; tail and wings are black with white edges.

Did you know? The Evening Grosbeak was mostly seen in western Canada until recent times when it moved east and north and can now be found in many parts of the Maritimes.

Voice: Call is a ringing cleer or clee-ip. When there is a flock of birds calling they sound like sleighbells.
Food: Seeds, insects various fruits and flower buds.
Nest/Eggs: Loosely woven cup of twigs and moss, lined with small roots. Conifer tree or shrub, in colonies. 3-4 eggs.

Backyard Feeder

Nesting Location

House Sparrow

Passer domesticus

Foot: Anisodactyl

Egg: Actual Size

Backyard Feeder

Birdhouse Nester

Nesting Location

Observation Calendar

J F M A M J J A S O N D

Male: Rich brown on head with white cheeks; wings and tail striped with black; two distinct white wing bands; rump grey; throat and chest black which turns grey at belly; bill black; feet and legs pink.

Female: Dull brown with buff chin, chest and belly; light buff coloured eyebrows and yellow/grey bill.

Did you know? In the mid-1800s, eight pairs of House Sparrows were brought to North America from Europe to help control cankerworms in crops. The first attempt failed, but this sparrow has now become one of the most common birds in cities and towns.

Voice: Repeated *chureep, chirup.*
Food: Insects, seed, grain, food waste.
Nest/Eggs: Takes over nests from other birds. Usually a large untidy ball of grass, weeds, some hair and feathers. 3-7 eggs.

Index